Berlitz®

Delhi

Front cover: in the Bu-Halima
garden at Humayun's Tomb
Right: a statue of the Hindu
deity, Ganesha

TOP 10 ATTRACTIONS

National Museum India's finest collection of Asian antiquities (page 45)

Jantar Mantar An 18th-century astronomical observatory (page 41)

Qutb Minar This 13th century complex marks the start of Islamic rule in North India (page 62)

Humayun's Tomb The elegant and imposing resting place of the second Moghul emperor, built in the 16th century (page 51)

Red Fort Once the seat of Moghul power and now a symbol of Delhi – and India (page 27)

Rajpath The Indian capital's ceremonial avenue is lined with grand state buildings (page 44)

Baha'i Temple Shaped like a huge lotus, this modern shrine never fails to impress (page 60)

Raj Ghat A simple and moving tribute to a great leader: Mahatma Gandhi (page 38)

Lodi Gardens In the midst of a congested city, these parklands are a welcome oasis (page 55)

Connaught Place The commercial heart of Delhi is home to a vast array of eateries, shops and offices (page 40)

A PERFECT DAY

8am — Lodi start

The crumbling 15th-century Afghan tombs in Lodi Gardens, an oasis of calm and greenery in south Delhi, provide a superb atmospheric venue for early morning yoga or simply a stroll.

Noon — Café break

When retail fatigue sets in, wander around the evocative medieval ruins of Hauz Khas gardens, set on the banks of a serene lake, or admire them from a rooftop café terrace: one of the hottest spots is Bohème (see page 111).

11am — Village shop

Browse the antique shops, hip clothes boutiques, designer furniture outlets, art galleries and ethnic jewellery stalls jammed into the old alleyways of Hauz Khas village.

1pm — Jama Masjid

The most resplendent vestige of Mughal Delhi is without doubt the red-sandstone and white-marble Jama Masjid mosque, whose vast domes dominate the skyline of the old city. Climb one of its lofty minarets for a matchless view over the surrounding rooftops.

9am — Breakfast at Sagar

There's no better way to fuel up for a full-on day's sightseeing than a proper south Indian breakfast at Sagar restaurant (see page 113) in the Defence Colony. Their iddlys are freshly steamed and fluffy, the chatni eye-poppingly tangy and the wadas totally scrumptious.

IN DELHI

3pm — Red Fort

Nerve centre of the illustrious Mughal Dynasty, Emperor Shah Jahan's Red Fort is among the world's most exquisite palace complexes and remains a poignant testament to the city's former glory. Enter via Lahore Gate and wonder at its massive presence while relaxing in the peaceful grounds.

9pm — Dinner

Located in a pair of old whitewashed haveli on the quieter southern edge of Delhi, Olive (see page 112) is one of Delhi's most glamorous places to dine. It serves pan-Mediterranean cuisine and the bill's worth it for the ambience and location – the terrace enjoys views of the nearby Qtub Minar complex.

2pm — Lunch

The perfect pit stop after a tour of the mosque is this legendary Old Delhi Mughlai joint. Don't let the downbeat strip lights and formica tables of Karim's (see page 108) put you off: their kebabs, chicken curries and piping hot rotis are melt-in-the-mouth.

4.30pm — High Tea

The Imperial Hotel (see page 134) off Connaught Place is a byword for colonial-era elegance, and the Atrium Tea Room is the ideal spot to sample its timeless charm – ideally over a cup of 'tippy golden flowery orange pekoe', India's finest tea.

6pm — Bollywood

Catch the latest Bollywood hit at one of the landmark movie houses on Connaught Place: the PVR Plaza, Odeon, or Regal.

CONTENTS

INTRODUCTION

Delhi thrives on being all things to all people, but the initial impact of all those things, and all those people, can be bewildering. One way to deal with this seemingly indecipherable maelstrom is to cut it into manageable morsels; eight different cities have stood here over the centuries and, like London, Delhi is effectively a vast collection of villages, each with a distinct identity and allure.

In common with those landing at altitude, first-time visitors are recommended to do as little as possible for the first couple of days, giving themselves a chance to settle in and take the pulse of the place before starting to move around. The disorientation that Delhi can deliver has not gone unnoticed by the city's less scrupulous travel agents and touts; weary travellers need to be on their guard from the word go. Booking your first night's accommodation in advance is highly recommended; failure to do so could lead to an adventure you'll be dining out on for years. It should be stressed that the threat is generally financial rather than physical, with charm the most effective weapon you're likely to be faced with.

Delhis Old and New

The city's most pronounced divide is between Old and New Delhi, but as the metropolis expands old borders are broken and ever newer Delhis demarcated. A large river, the Yamuna, bisects Delhi north to south, but many visitors leave without seeing it. A polluted and unloved waterway which most Delhiites do their best to ignore, the river is lined by many of the city's slums, or *jhuggis*, which are home to a quarter of Delhi's 15 million people. The 'Yamuna Action Plan', a massive

A man prays at the Jama Masjid (Grand Mosque)

Going greener

All public transport has run on compressed natural gas since 2001, a radical and much-lauded move which has significantly improved the quality of Delhi's air, though exhaust fumes and gridlocked traffic remain an inescapable feature of life in the city.

restoration project bilaterally funded by the Indian and Japanese governments in the 1990s, met with little success, and its successor, YAPII, is faring little better.

Thanks at least in part to its role as host of the 2010 Commonwealth Games, public transport and infrastructure in Delhi are slowly improving. Auto-rickshaws, the Indian answer to the Thai tuk tuk, are slowly being phased out in favour of a new fleet of sleek, green, low-floored cluster buses, as well as the city's steadily growing metro system. The three underground lines so far opened are already so heavily used that previously packed bus routes have had to be diverted away from areas served by the new trains.

Unesco has called Delhi 'the world's largest heritage site', with over 60,000 recognised monuments. The most celebrated have been well maintained, with Humayun's Tomb in particular having been beautifully restored. Many, however, are less well preserved, and now stand surrounded by more recent developments, leading to chance encounters with ancient history when you least expect it. Some fine examples of such scattered treasures are those in Lodi Gardens, perhaps Delhi's most elegant park, and a great place to go when it's all getting a bit much.

A political city

Delhi's political supremacy lends the city much of its flavour. Visitors will often hear, and then see, swooping convoys of politicians' white Ambassadors (a locally made copy of the 1940s Morris Oxford), red lights flashing and sirens screaming from their rooftops, preceded by police escorts riding white Royal

Enfields (copies of a 1940s British motorcycle), the pomp on display as anachronistic as the vehicles used.

The vagaries of the Indian political landscape are well known, with celebrities as persuasive as policies, but the effect of politics on Delhi's cultural life is less well documented. A long tradition, and now rigid expectation, of political gratuities has been a definite factor in Delhi's stunted growth as an international entertainment venue, though recent years have seen increased public protest against the capital's ingrained culture of corruption.

Variety, colour and change

The politicians have presided over a sharp rise in living standards, especially among the middle classes. Concrete evidence of this boom is springing up all over town. An eclectic exuberance of architectural styles can be seen liberally sprinkled through Delhi's more upmarket residential

Select City Walk shopping mall

An ambassador at the Secretariat

districts, with Spanish villas abutting crenellated castles and Renaissance mansions face to face with the starkest of minimalist façades. These clashing tastes reflect the diverse demography of Delhi. The post-Partition influx of Punjabis probably had the most profound effect on the city's character, but Delhi's continued daily digestion of immigrants makes it a city of constantly changing character and colour. While Delhi is 85 percent Hindu, most of the world's faiths have a home here. Major religious landmarks include the Sikh Gurudwara Bangla Sahib near Connaught Place, the city's commercial hub, the Muslim Jama Masjid in Old Delhi, the Hindu Birla Mandir to the west and the Baha'i Lotus and Akshardham Temples to the south.

The visual ramifications of all this variety are certainly eye-catching. You'll see ash-smeared Hindus, their foreheads pasted white and a red smear bisecting their eyes, and extravagantly turbaned Sikhs, a white chinstrap holding their freshly set beard in place on their way to work. An orthodox Jain may pass you by, a white cloth covering his mouth for fear of inhaling and thus harming a living creature, sweeping the path before him to be sure he does no harm with his feet. And you might glimpse a Sadhu, a Hindu aesthete who has renounced all worldly possessions and is often clad in saffron robes.

The city's sophisticates, meanwhile, no longer need to travel abroad for their favourite designer labels, the fashion world having come to town in no mean way. Most five-star hotels feature luxury boutiques, while the shopping malls to the city's south offer goods and an experience comparable to anywhere in the Western world. Further options for retail rhapsody abound, with bargains in all shapes and sizes waiting to be unearthed. Handicrafts, fabrics, clothes, shoes, bags, jewellery and books are all worth seeking out.

Indian food reflects a blend of cultures, and what a sumptuous spread it is. Rich Punjabi and Mughlai dishes dominate, but India's choicest cuisines are all here, from the Tibet-derived dishes of the far North to the fragrant fusions of the South, and from the sweet savouries of Gujarat to Mumbai's street snacks, all washed down with a cup of *masala chai*. In addition, restaurants serving fancy international gourmet cuisine are opening all the time.

The variety even extends to the weather, as you might expect from a city that is situated midway between a desert and the highest mountains in the world. While the searingly hot and humid summers might come as no surprise, the freezing winters catch even the locals out, with as many deaths per year from the cold as the heat. Perhaps this in part explains the resilience of the population, and the slow pace of cultural change; when one Delhi cricketer coming home after playing abroad for a number of years – a period of great expansion in the city's infrastructure – was asked what had changed, his reply was 'Nothing'. In many ways he was probably right, and perhaps always will be.

At the temple in Hauz Khas

A BRIEF HISTORY

Delhi is thought to be the site of 'Indraprastha', first mentioned in the epic tale of Indian history, the *Mahabharata*, which some scholars have dated to the 5th century BC. Its strategic location as the gateway to the Gangetic plains guaranteed the city an influential role in the country's development, and successive dynasties have attempted to make it their own. Archeological finds tell us that the location has been continuously inhabited since at least 1000BC.

Delhi's history is a tale of not one city but at least eight successive ones in different locations in the same general area. The first was Lal Kot, established in the 11th century by Raja Anangpal of Kanauj, near the present-day Qutb Minar. Anangpal was the leader of the Tomara Rajputs, one of the many warrior clans fighting for control of northern and western India at the time. Another Rajput clan, the Chauhans, succeeded the Tomaras. They expanded the borders of the city and renamed it Qila Rai Pithora.

The Afghans attack

The job of dislodging the Rajputs fell to the Afghans, who had been making incursions into northern India since the reign of Mahmud of Ghazni at the beginning of the 11th century. Mahmud crashed through present-day Pakistan and the Punjab before finally running out of energy just north of Delhi.

Some 160 years later, another Afghan ruler, Muhammad of Ghor, launched further raids on the subcontinent. In the face of the new Afghan threat, the various Rajput clans of northwestern India patched together a hastily formed alliance and in 1191 defeated Muhammad's forces at Tarain, 130km (80 miles) north of Delhi and scene of many a notable battle since. The victory was short-lived, however. A year later

Muhammad returned with superior forces, and this time got the better of the Rajputs.

The Slave Dynasty (1206–90)

Perhaps only in it for the chase, Muhammad headed back to Afghanistan in his hour of glory, leaving his Turkish slave-general, Qutb-ud-din Aibak, in charge of his newly acquired city. Following Muhammad's death in 1206, Qutb-ud-din became first sultan of Delhi, but after just four years on the throne, a fatal polo accident put an end to his reign; he's best remembered as the man who started construction of the Qutb Minar, a Delhi landmark. Qutb-ud-din's son took over, but was soon replaced by his far more effective brother-in-law, Iltutmish. Shams-ud-din, as he came to be known, ruled for 25 years, and added further touches to the Qutb Minar. The only slave ruler of note to come after him was Sultan Balban, who ruled in ruthless fashion from 1246 to 1266. His habit of killing anyone he regarded as a rival to the throne meant that there was nobody around to take over after his death. The Khalji Afghan-Turks filled the power vacuum.

Qutb Minar

The Khalji and Tughlaq Dynasties (1290–1414)

Cruel but cultured, the Khaljis' main man was Ala-ud-din,

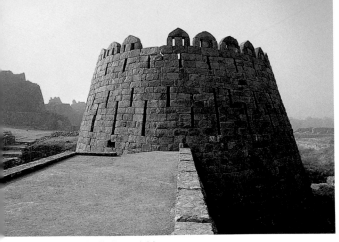

Tughlaqabad's formidable ramparts

who ruled from 1296 to 1316. It was under his despotic regime that Siri, Delhi's second city, took shape, of which only a reservoir – at Hauz Khas – still survives.

Ala-ud-din was succeeded by the first of the Tughlaq rulers, Ghazi Malik, who just had time to build Delhi's third city, the still imposing Tughlaqabad, before being murdered by his own son. Muhammad-bin-Tughlaq kept Tughlaqabad as his capital, but nonetheless saw fit to build a city of his own between Siri and Qila Rai Pithora. This was called Jahanpanah, city number four. The once-great empire gradually declined under his erratic rule, and in 1351 Feroz Shah Tughlaq came to power. A far more moderate character, Feroz Shah made the best of what he'd been given, and, true to Tughlaq form, built himself a self-named city, Ferozabad. The remains of this fifth city can still be seen close to today's New Delhi. The 26 years following Feroz Shah's death were marked by squabbling and instability, the lowlight coming when Tamerlane, the famed sultan of Samarkand, ransacked the city in 1398.

The Sayyids and the Lodis (1414–1526)

It was a much-reduced empire that the Sayyids inherited from the Tughlaqs. The 37-year Sayyid dynasty is remembered today chiefly for the magnificence of its rulers' mausoleums, fine examples of which can still be seen in South Delhi's Lodi Gardens.

The Lodis did much to regain land lost since Tamerlane's raid, but never managed to see eye to eye with the Afghan nobles. In 1526, the Afghans invited Babur, the Moghul ruler of Kabul and a descendant of both Tamerlane and Ghengis Khan, to attack Delhi. So began the era of Moghul rule.

The Moghuls (1526–1857)

Now seen as perhaps the greatest period in Delhi's history, the Moghul dynasty got off to a somewhat shaky start. After a promising four-year period under Babur, his son Humayun took over, but made such a hash of things that in 1539 he was forced into exile. Sher Shah, an Afghan noble who had been ruling Bihar for some time, took over, and during his short reign managed to complete Delhi's sixth city, started by Humayun, which is today known as Purana Qila, Sher Shah's death was followed by a period of instability, setting the stage for the return of Humayun, who re-took the city in 1555.

The century covering the reigns of Akbar, Jehangir and Shah Jahan (1556–1658) was marked by stability and outstanding contributions to the arts. Akbar, successor to Humayun, was perhaps the greatest and certainly the fairest of the Moghul emperors. His military intelligence meant that all lingering remains of Afghan rule were removed, while his sense of justice saw Hindus being not only tolerated but welcomed

Humayun's Fall

Just seven months after returning to the throne, Humayun died after falling down the steps of his library in Purana Qila whilst hurrying to answer the call to prayer.

into the court as advisers and administrators, as well as wives and concubines – a first under Muslim rule.

Akbar was succeeded by his son Jehangir, who exhibited less interest in the affairs of the court, spending most of his time in the cool of Kashmir. Shah Jahan, the next in line, was altogether more ambitious. He not only extended the borders of the empire still further, but also instigated the construction of the most lauded of all Moghul monuments, the Taj Mahal, as well as Shahjahanabad, Delhi's seventh city and the basis of today's Old Delhi, complete with its magnificent Red Fort and Jama Masjid.

A stroke in 1657 led to premature reports of the ruler's death, and thus an unseemly squabble began between his four sons over the vexed question of succession. Aurangzeb eventually came out on top, and began his reign by imprisoning his father in Agra Fort; Shah Jahan was to remain there for the last eight years of his life.

Aurangzeb (reigned 1658–1707) is widely seen as the last of the great Moghuls, but it was during his 50-year reign that the empire began its terminal decline. His military ambitions consumed a large part of the state's resources, while his austere religious beliefs saw him desecrate Hindu temples, replacing them with mosques and thus alienating the majority of his subjects. A period of instability followed his death in 1707; by 1739 the Moghul hold on the empire had grown so weak that a Persian king, Nadir Shah, successfully took control of Delhi in an attack lasting no more than two hours. As well as contending with the increasingly confident Marathas, champions of the Hindu cause, Delhi also had to vie with other parts of the empire for supremacy, with both Hyderabad and Awadh (present-day Lucknow) emerging as significant seats of power.

Those two cities eventually broke away from the Moghul empire, whose ruler was left with little but the districts in Delhi's immediate vicinity. Much of the rest of India was now controlled by the Marathas, and increasingly, the British, in the guise of the East India Company. The year 1761 saw another battle for control of Delhi take place, this time between an Afghan army and the Marathas, who were eventually vanquished after a bloody two-month siege at Panipat, north of Delhi. While the Moghuls were ostensibly in power until 1857, they were emperors in name only; the real power by this time lay elsewhere.

Shah Jahan on his throne

The British (1803–1947)

The British East India Company had gradually been assuming control of parts of the subcontinent during the latter half of the 18th century. In 1803, they went to war with the Marathas just east of Delhi. Victorious, the British then marched on Delhi, placed the Moghul emperor under their protection and installed an administrator, the so-called British Resident, who slowly took over the running of the city

Social unrest, fuelled by insensitive handling of Hindu traditions, had been bubbling away since the defeat of the Marathas, and came to a head in 1857. The Indian Mutiny, or War of Independence as it is now known in India, took the British completely unawares, and continued for the best part of a year until reinforcements arrived and quelled the disturbance. Alarmed by their close call, the British response was heavy-handed: they executed many of the perceived instigators of the revolt and banished all Muslims from the city for two years. The East India Company was also wound up, and power handed over to the Crown, which ruled through a viceroy. Calcutta (now Kolkata) was the capital of British India, but Delhi continued to thrive during the prosperous latter half of the 19th century thanks to its strategic location.

The Peacock Throne

The splendour of the Peacock Throne reflected the might of its first occupant, Shah Jahan (1592–1666), builder of the Taj Mahal, Red Fort and Shahjahanabad. Backed by two sculpted peacocks, their tail feathers resplendently fanned, the solid-gold throne was inlaid with sapphires, rubies, emeralds, pearls and other precious stones (including the famous Kohinoor diamond) to create a display so colourful that it was said to represent life itself. Shah Jahan gave the throne pride of place in the Diwan-i-Am in Delhi's Red Fort. It was, perhaps, the ultimate seat of power.

But this symbol of imperial power lasted for little more than a century. In 1738, the Persian Nadir Shah attacked the Moghul empire, departing in 1739 with the Peacock Throne as his trophy. The throne was later destroyed in the mayhem that followed Nadir Shah's assassination. Over the years since then, many copies have been produced in Iran, where the term 'Peacock Throne' became an alternative moniker for the monarchy itself.

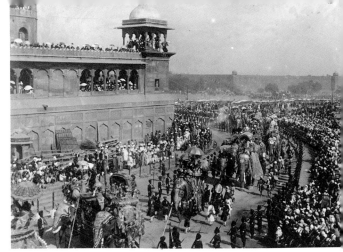

Edward VII's Coronation Durbar in Delhi, 1903

At the coronation of King George V in 1911, it was announced that Delhi would be the new capital of India. Work began immediately on New Delhi, an area of broad, tree-lined avenues and public buildings designed to surpass in their grandeur all that had gone before them, and thus reflect the supremacy of colonial rule. New Delhi was formally inaugurated in 1931, but the extent to which the British had misjudged the longevity of their empire soon became apparent. In 1945, weakened by two world wars and coming under increasing pressure from Mahatma Gandhi's non-violent freedom movement, the British announced plans for India's independence. The viceroy, Lord Mountbatten decreed that India would achieve independence on 15 August 1947.

Independence, Partition and aftermath

The British decided that the only way to resolve persistent Hindu–Muslim tensions was to divide the two groups

At the Indira Ghandi
Memorial Museum

physically by drawing lines through west and east India to create two new countries: present-day Pakistan and Bangladesh. The horror of Partition has been well documented, and lives on in the memories of many Delhiites today. The Punjab saw some of the worst of the violence. In some cases, entire train-loads of Muslim or Hindus refugees were ambushed and killed.

Partition changed the face of Delhi. The previously Muslim-majority city became one of Punjabi immigrants (both Hindu and Sikh). Whereas the city had been clustered around Delhis New and Old, the new arrivals camped on the city's periphery. In doing so they unwittingly laid the foundations for the shape of the modern metropolis today, an outline made concrete by the extensive building programmes of the 1950s. Communal problems did not end with Partition. When Indira Gandhi was assassinated by her Sikh bodyguards in 1984, largely Hindu mobs went on the rampage in Delhi, killing as many Sikhs as they could find.

The city has prospered, however, attracting countless newcomers hoping to get their slice of the cake. Infrastructure has struggled to adapt to the city's burgeoning size, as have attitudes. Some see the city as superficial, a place where national institutions have their headquarters but where nothing much seems to get done. *Outlook* magazine has described Delhi as 'All HQ, no IQ', neatly encapsulating the challenges ahead for this vibrant metropolis.

Historical Landmarks

1000BC Earliest archaeological evidence of settlement in Delhi area.

AD700–1192 Rajputs rule in Delhi (Tomaras and Chauhans).

1191 Rai Pithora Chauhan crushes Muhammed-bin-Sam at Tarain.

1192 Second battle of Tarain. Chauhan killed. Qutb-ud-din Aibak becomes governor of Delhi (sultan from 1206).

1211 Iltutmish becomes sultan. Completes the Qutb Minar.

1296–1316 Reign of Ala-ud-din. Construction of Siri.

1320s Ghazi Malik builds Tughlaqabad.

1354 Feroz Shah Tughlaq builds Ferozabad.

1398 Delhi taken by Tamerlane.

1526 Babur invades India and defeats Ibrahim Lodi at Panipat. Beginning of Moghul dynasty.

1530 Humayun comes to the throne; exiled by Sher Shah in 1539.

1555 Humayun regains power.

1569 Akbar founds Fatehpur Sikri.

1632 Shah Jahan begins Taj Mahal.

1658–1707 Reign of Aurangzeb.

1739 Nadir Shah sacks Delhi; takes Peacock Throne.

1803 Establishment of East India Company rule.

1857 Indian Mutiny (War of Independence). End of Moghul rule. British Crown takes over administration, with Calcutta (Kolkata) as capital.

1866 Railways come to Delhi.

1877 Queen Victoria made empress of India.

1911 Delhi becomes capital of India.

1947 Independence and Partition.

1948 Mahatma Gandhi is assassinated in Delhi.

1951 India becomes a republic. First general elections.

1984 Indira Gandhi assassinated in Delhi.

2002 First line of metro system opened.

2005 Delhi's population crosses 15 million mark.

2010 Delhi hosts the Commonwealth Games.

2011 Anti-corruption rallies in the capital make international headlines.

WHERE TO GO

For many visitors, it is the experience of simply being in Delhi, rather than any one particular sight, which lingers longest in the memory. This is especially true of Old Delhi, as condensed a mass of teeming humanity as exists anywhere in the world. As its name implies, it's also where many of Delhi's most historic landmarks are found, and probably the best place to begin touring the city.

Having negotiated Old Delhi, the rest of the capital feels a whole lot more relaxed. New Delhi is epitomised by wide, tree-lined avenues, and is home to elegant whitewashed bungalows and the city's political elite. Contained within this area are a number of world-class cultural experiences, from museums honouring the lives of some of Delhi's greatest residents to beautifully maintained gardens dotted with fine Moghul monuments, plus temples, mosques and churches.

OLD DELHI

Old Delhi was originally the walled city of **Shahjahanabad**, built by the Moghul emperor Shah Jahan in 1648. The old city has, of course, expanded greatly over the centuries, but the places of most interest to visitors lie in a fairly compact area within the original boundaries. Most of the old walls have gone, but some of the entry gates survive, and form invaluable landmarks in this most congested of cityscapes. The only people who make real inroads on any motorised form of transport are the boldest of scooter riders.

Other modern-day amenities, such as running water and mains electricity, have also run into trouble in the narrow

Humayun's Tomb

The Red Fort's Lahore Gate

lanes. Evidence of this can be seen everywhere you look, with alarming spaghetti junctions of cables running amok at first-floor level, and water pipes jutting out when you least expect them. Among all this chaos, some sort of organisation prevails. This was until 1947 a predominantly Muslim city, and the arrangement of its markets owes much to the Middle Eastern *souq*. Goods for sale are grouped into specific areas, so while one street will sell nothing but stationery, the next will be lined with shops selling kitchen utensils.

The narrow nature of Old Delhi's *galis* (alleyways) means that walking is really the only way to get around, although taking a cycle rickshaw can make sense for longer journeys. It's best to get the walking done as early in the day as possible, before it gets too hot, and then to spend the rest of the day relaxing in the peaceful grounds of the Red Fort. If you're coming from New Delhi, the easiest way to gain access to the old city is by metro, just three short stops from Connaught Place.

Red Fort (Lal Qila)

The **Red Fort** ❶ (Lal Qila; Tue–Sun sunrise–sunset; charge) takes its name from the colour of its massively imposing sandstone walls – almost 2km (1.25 miles) in length – which can be seen all over Old Delhi. Completed in 1648 by Shah Jahan, the fort originally stood on the banks of the Yamuna River, which filled its moat; the river has now receded to almost a kilometre (just over 0.5 mile) away, and the moat has been dry for decades. The fort's entrance is via **Lahore Gate**, one of India's most emotive landmarks. The area outside the gate has seen crowds gather throughout history to be addressed by their leader, and the Indian prime minister still speaks from here on Independence Day. The ornate original gate is obscured by the solid bastion added by the defence-minded Aurangzeb, Shah Jahan's son and successor.

Having entered the fort and escaped the commercial cacophony of Old Delhi, you may be dismayed to come across

Old Delhi's Havelis

While few of Delhi's dignitaries would choose to live in Old Delhi today, there were once a large number of nobleman's havelis (residences) within the city walls. Each one took the form of a large, high-walled enclosure housing a series of apartments separated by shady courtyards, gardens and waterways. Although many of them are of great historical importance -- Jawaharlal Nehru, India's first prime minister, was married in one, for example – they are badly neglected and on the point of ruin. One of the better examples is that of Hakeem Ahsanullah Khan, close to the Excelsior Cinema. An idea of the kind of opulence enjoyed by its former inhabitants is given by the abandoned Cadillac close to the entrance, and by the Turkish hammam-style baths. The haveli complex was originally much larger than it looks today, and would have encompassed the cinema hall and several of the other surrounding buildings.

yet more shops as soon as you get through the gate. There is, however, a historical precedent for their existence, for it was here in **Chatta Chowk** that the royal bazaar was housed, stocking items designed to take the royal family's fancy. On the right as you leave the bazaar is **Naubat Khanna** (Drum House), which marks the point at which visiting nobles were asked to dismount from their elephants. This was also where the court musicians would assemble five times a day to honour their emperor.

On entering the adjacent courtyard you'll be rewarded by the sight of the elegant **Diwan-i-Am** (Hall of Public Audiences), which was one of many buildings looted by British troops in the wake of the 1857 uprising, when the enclosure was commandeered as barracks. The Hall is also where the emperor would come to listen to the affairs of his subjects, seated on a raised throne at the back. Justice was dispensed quickly with executioners armed with all manner of axes, clubs, swords and even poisonous snakes standing ready to carry out the emperor's wishes. The inlaid marble panels behind the throne were restored in the early 1900s, and hint at the opulence of the original decor, which would have included satin curtains and Persian rugs, with a thin layer of highly decorated plaster covering the walls and pillars.

Leave the hall by following the path to your left when looking at the throne pedestal, and you'll enter the fort's inner sanctum, an area into which only the most senior of nobles would have been allowed. The path takes you past two white marble pavilions. The gardens around

Heart of India

The Red Fort, viewed by many as the heart of India, has great symbolic significance. Each year on 15 August (Independence Day) the prime minister addresses his people from here. It was only in 2003 that the Indian Army handed over control of the fort to the tourist authorities.

Keeping the pavilions spic and span

them, and those throughout the fort, were originally laid out in the symmetrical Persian *charbagh* style, but were callously dug up by the British. In their heyday these gardens were traversed by water channels known as the 'streams of paradise', with water pouring from the pavilion rooftops (designed to replicate the monsoon) and candles lit at night to highlight the effect.

The octagonal tower in the far corner was Shah Jahan's private office, but it was seriously damaged in 1857 and remains closed. Immediately to the right is Aurangzeb's **Moti Masjid** (Pearl Mosque), built in 1659, though sadly it's currently closed to the public so you can't enjoy its exquisite interior decor. Passing the Royal Baths, or Hammam, you'll come to the centrepiece of Shah Jahan's palace, the **Diwan-i-Khas** (Hall of Private Audiences).

The hall's interior was originally dominated by the legendary Peacock Throne (see page 20), a solid-gold masterpiece encrusted with precious jewels, chief among them the equally legendary Koh-i-noor diamond, which was taken to Tehran

Jama Masjid

by Nadir Shah in 1739. From the Hindu-style *chatris* (small domes) on its rooftop to the exquisite decoration of its interior and original silver ceiling, the hall enchanted one visitor so much that he was moved to line the walls with the famous Persian couplet, composed by the great 14th-century Indian poet Amir Khusrau, that translates as: 'If there be a paradise on earth, this is it, this is it, this is it.'

Shah Jahan built a series of small palaces along the exterior wall overlooking the river, and these make up the remainder of the fort's significant buildings. Next to the Diwan-i-Khas is **Khas Mahal**, the emperor's private palace. The three rooms were used for worship, sleeping and dressing respectively. The fine marble *jali* which bridges the water channel in the third room is a superb example of this type of intricate pierced-stone screen, widely used to dissipate heat.

Next along is the **Rang Mahal** (Palace of Colours), for-merly the living quarters of the emperor's principal wife. Its presumably once colourful interior was badly defaced when the palace was used as an officers' barracks by the British Army. Some of the mirror-inlaid ceiling remains, however, and the effect produced when candles were lit at night can still be imagined. Last but not least of the surviving palaces is the **Mumtaz Mahal** (Palace of Jewels), originally used by the court's harem. Today it is home to a collection of weapons, textiles, carpets and scenes of life in the palace.

There is a sound-and-light show at the fort (Tue–Sun), which receives mixed reviews. Check with the tourist office for the latest schedule, but the English-language programme is generally at 9pm in summer (May–Aug), 8.30pm in Feb–Apr and Sept–Oct, and 7.30pm in from Nov–Jan; a fee is charged.

Jama Masjid (Friday Mosque)

A couple of kilometres southwest of the Red Fort is the magnificent **Jama Masjid** ❷ (open to visitors from 30 minutes after sunrise until noon, and then again from 1.45pm until 30 minutes before sunset; free; Rs200 for a camera permit). Remove your shoes before entering, and anyone wearing shorts or a skirt will be given a length of cloth with which to cover their legs. The mosque's three gateways, their scale and splendour intended to remind worshippers that they are entering a place of God, lead to the 25,000-capacity courtyard. The gate to the east was originally only for use by the emperor and his family, and even today is open only on Fridays. Such is the mosque's size that the platform in front of the central tank was used by an extra prayer leader to relay the actions

Sunday walk

If you're around on Sunday mornings, a great way to see some of the less easily accessible architectural and cultural highlights of Chandni Chowk and its backstreets is to sign up for one of the old city's popular Heritage Walks (www.delhiheritage-walks.com).

of the imam to the worshippers on the western side, too far away to make him out.

There is a small shed on the northwestern side of the court-yard, where for a small fee you'll be shown a hair from the Prophet's beard, a sandal and his footprint. The minaret in the opposite corner can be climbed for a small fee, although women on their own may be discouraged from doing so. The views of the top of the Red Fort and New Delhi make the climb more than worthwhile.

Chandni Chowk and the spice market

Chandni Chowk ❸, the street which runs due west from the entrance to the Red Fort, was once renowned throughout Asia, and had a canal running down its centre. While it may have lost some of its former glory, it still makes for a fascinat-ing spectacle. At the far, western end of the thoroughfare next

The bustle of the Old City off Chandni Chowk

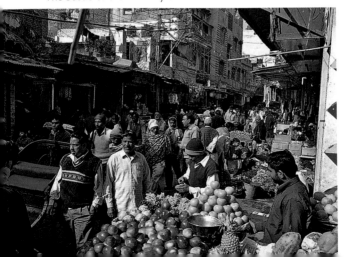

to the Fatehpuri Mosque lies the pungent-smelling wholesale spice market, Khari Baoli, the largest of its kind in India. The roof of the covered section, Gadodia Market, is a good place from which to look out over Old Delhi, giving an impression of the city's size and concentration.

Barbers near Chandni Chowk

Chandni Chowk is also home to India's oldest library, the **Hardayal Municipal Public Library**, housed in a recently restored colonial-style building roughly halfway up on the right-hand side (with the Red Fort behind you). In colonial times, Englishmen posted to India brought a large number of books with them, many of which they left behind on returning home. These formed the nucleus of the library's collection, which was established in 1862 and has since grown to include titles in Hindi, Persian, Sanskrit, Arabic and Urdu. Of the 170,000 books inside, more than 6,000 are over 100 years old.

If this brief introduction to Old Delhi leaves you wanting more, head by foot into the area south of Chandni Chowk. Take any left turn (if the Red Fort's behind you) to find the jewellery and wedding bazaars. Colourful and glitzy, as well as unbelievably narrow, they run more or less parallel to Chandni Chowk. Better still, just let yourself get lost as you wander around this tangle of lanes. When it's time to leave, simply ask for directions to the Red Fort.

Birds of pray

Also close to Chandni Chowk, on the main road opposite the Red Fort, the Lal Mandir Jain Temple is not only beautiful but also has a bird hospital.

NORTH DELHI

Kashmiri Gate and Civil Lines

The northern entrance to Shahjahanabad was through **Kashmiri Gate**, the city's grandest gateway and the only one to have two arches. It was from Kashmiri Gate that the ruling family would leave to spend summer in the cool of Kashmir. It was also the scene of some of the Mutiny's heaviest fighting. After gathering on the Ridge behind and breaching the walls with cannonball fire, British forces attacked Kashmiri Gate on 14 September 1857, desperate to regain control of the city from the mutineers. Fighting continued for six days – evidence of cannonball fire can still be seen on the gate – until the British finally triumphed despite heavy losses.

The area immediately to the north of Old Delhi, known as Civil Lines, was where the British were based prior to the creation of New Delhi, and there are still some interesting reminders of the Raj here. Foremost of these is the **Dara Shikoh Library/Old Residency**, in the grounds of the Indraprastha University on Lothian Road, originally the library of Shah Jahan's favourite son, which became home to the British Resident in 1803. Somewhat unusually, Sir David Ochterlony, the Resident who initially moved in, first built a complete mansion on top of the original Moghul building, traces of which can still be seen inside and to the rear. The building now houses a small **Archeological Museum** (open Mon–Fri 10am–5pm charge).

Close to Kashmiri Gate lies Delhi's oldest church, **St James's Church** ❹, which was built by the legendary James Skinner (*see box*) in 1836, allegedly in fulfillment of a vow made as he lay wounded on a battlefield. Skinner's grave still rests in front of the altar, while his family tombstones may be seen outside to the north of the building. The church itself is

St James's Church

a classical Western design, the plan in the Greek Cross configuration. Badly damaged during the Mutiny, it underwent restoration work in 1865, and the stained-glass windows were enhanced in 1996.

Heading north from Kashmiri Gate, immediately behind the unattractive Interstate Bus terminal, lies the once magnificent formal garden of **Qudsia Bagh**. Built by Qudsia Begum in 1748 for her lover and later husband, the Moghul emperor Muhammad Shah, it originally contained a palace, mosque, canals, waterfalls, rose beds and fruit trees. While it still retains a peaceful dignity and is a pleasant place to while away an hour or so, much of the site was taken over by the bus terminal, and today the buildings and tennis courts have been commandeered by the Masonic Lodge. Under the British, the park was open to Indians only in the morning as it was reserved for tennis-playing Europeans after midday

Close to the gardens, on Qudsia Road, the beautifully restored **Nicholson Cemetery** is home to the graves of some of the British soldiers killed in the 1857 Mutiny, including the notoriously bloodthirsty Brigadier General John Nicholson, who was shot dead during the storming of the Kashmiri Gate.

The Ridge

Visitors with a keen interest in British India should head for the **Ridge ❺**, a scrub-covered hillock which was originally hunting territory and remains undeveloped today. Moving along Rani Jhansi Road from south to north, the highlights in order of appearance include the **Mutiny Memorial**, built by the British in 1863 to commemorate their victory over the

Skinner's exploits

One of the great personalities of 19th-century India was James Skinner, born in 1778 to a Scottish soldier named Hercules and a Hindu Rajput mother. Although eager to pursue his father's line of work, young James was refused entry to the British Army because of his Indian mother. Undeterred, he took to fighting for Indian Maratha warlords instead, eventually forming his own irregular cavalry corps under the maharaja of Gwalior and enjoying outstanding success in battle.

The Marathas then decided to take on the British but ultimately lost, at which point Skinner was invited to rejoin the East India Company's army, in which he again formed his own cavalry regiment: the illustrious 'Skinner's Horse', a unit of which still serves in the Indian Army today (as a tank regiment). Although chiefly remembered for his exploits on the battlefield, this colourful character later wrote a number of volumes in Persian, and came to be known as 'Sikander Sahib' after Alexander the Great. He died in 1841 at the age of 63.

mutineers, and interesting for the conflicting points of view reflected in the inscriptions on it; an ancient, if somewhat dilapidated **Ashokan Pillar**, brought here by the Tughlaqs in 1356; and the **Flagstaff Tower**, which commemorates the spot where British women and child refugees fleeing the Mutiny in Delhi first took shelter.

Kashmiri Gate

A kilometre (about 0.5 mile) west of the Ridge Road, just off the main Trunk Road, lies **Roshanara Garden**, built by Emperor Shah Jahan's youngest daughter as a pleasure garden and site for her own tomb. Much modified from the elegant original, the park is now home to the Roshanara Club and boasts a well-maintained cricket pitch. The British did away with many of the original monuments, so today only the princess's tomb itself is still standing.

Coronation Memorial

A further 5km (3 miles) to the north is the **Coronation Memorial**. This was the site of the three biggest durbar ceremonies under British rule, the first to pronounce Queen Victoria as empress of India in 1877, followed by the 1903 celebration of Edward VII's accession to the throne and finally the 1911 coronation of George V. The area's British connections meant that when Delhi's remaining British statues were rounded up after independence, it was here that they were put out to graze.

Most impressive of these is the statue of George V at his coronation – the robe he wore for the occasion rippling behind him – which was originally located at India Gate (see page 43). Sadly, many of these monuments are in a somewhat sorry state, and this, together with the abandoned air of the place, can make it difficult to conjure up its illustrious past.

Raj Ghat

To the south and east of the Red Fort lie the cremation sites of some of 20th-century India's greatest leaders. Furthest to the south is a simple black-marble platform, known as **Raj Ghat ❻** (daily 5.30am–7pm; free), where Mahatma Gandhi was cremated following his assassination in 1948. The **Gandhi Memorial Museum** (Tue–Sat and alternate Sundays 9.30am–5.30pm; free) here houses a display of Gandhi's personal belongings and has a library of recordings of his speeches.

Campus history

Close to the Flagstaff Tower is the campus of Delhi University. The building that today houses the university vice chancellor's offices was once an official guesthouse for British military officers. In what is now the office of the registrar, the young Louis Mountbatten, later to become the last viceroy of British India, proposed to Edwina Ashley. She accepted and was to become Countess Mountbatten, the vice-reine. A plaque in the room commemorates the event.

To the north is Shanti Vana, Forest of Peace, the family cremation site for the Nehru/Gandhi dynasty; India's first prime minister, Jawaharlal Nehru, was cremated here in 1964, followed by his grandson Sanjay Gandhi in 1980, his daughter Indira Gandhi in 1984 and elder grandson, Rajiv, in 1991. To the north again is **Vijay Ghat**, Victory Ghat, where Nehru's successor, Prime Minister Lal Bahadur Shastri, was cremated.

To the southwest of Raj Ghat are the last remaining traces of **Ferozabad**, Delhi's fifth city, built by Feroz Shah Tughlaq in 1354. A few traces of the city's fort, Feroz Shah Kotla, still remain, topped by the impressive 13-m (43-ft) high **Ashoka Pillar**. Dating to the 3rd century BC, it was installed in Ambala by the emperor Ashoka, but moved here by Feroz Shah. There is another similarly old pillar on the Ridge (see page 37), but this one is in far better condition.

Roshanara Gardens

NEW DELHI

For a city that was inaugurated as recently as 1931, New Delhi has developed extraordinarily quickly. Edwin Lutyens, New Delhi's principal architect, was caught between the wishes of King George V, who wanted a city built in the Moghul style of Old Delhi's finest monuments, and his own passionate dislike of such Oriental styles. The result is largely classical in appearance, but with liberal application of Indian Moghul motifs in deference to the king's wishes.

While the centre of political power lies around the parliament buildings, ministries and president's residence – all strung out along Rajpath between India Gate and Rashtrapati Bhawan – the commercial hub of New Delhi is Connaught Place, a couple of kilometres to the north, to which all roads in New Delhi seem to lead. Spreading from this original nucleus in all directions are the later and less grandiose

Gandhi Memorial at Raj Ghat

additions to Lutyens's Delhi, with many of the city's inhabitants now living on the previously ignored east bank of the Yamuna River. The principal attractions of New Delhi all lie due south of Connaught Place. Few visitors venture to the east or west of town.

Connaught Place and around

Connaught Place ❼, or 'CP' as it's commonly known, basically comprises two concentric circles, the inner one known as Connaught Place, with elegant (albeit somewhat crumbling) colonnaded neoclassical buildings surrounding a circle of open grass, the outer as Connaught Circus. The shops and offices between the two are divided into a series of lettered blocks, and form the heart of New Delhi's commercial district. Many international brands have stores here, and there's also an excellent range of places to eat. Rajiv Chowk, the metro station beneath Connaught Place, is the central hub of the new railway system, emphasising CP's status as New Delhi's centre of attention.

A short distance south of Connaught Place on Sansad Marg lies **Jantar Mantar** ❽ (sunrise–sunset; charge), a fascinating collection of astrological instruments built in 1724–5 by the maharaja of Jaipur. The garden setting of this observatory is dominated by the central sundial, to the south of which lie instruments capable of ascertaining the position and altitude of the sun and the planets. On the right as you enter is a contraption which calculates the time in four of the world's time zones when Delhi time reaches noon – ingenious to say the least.

The architects of New Delhi

Born in London in 1869, Edwin Landseer Lutyens was known principally for his work on English country houses prior to his appointment as chief architect of New Delhi. Concerned that he may become overburdened by the vast scale of the project, Lutyens insisted that Herbert Baker be appointed his assistant. The two had first met in the offices of Ernest George, a British administrator in South Africa; it was Baker's work on the Union Buildings in Pretoria, South Africa's seat of government, that had convinced Lutyens that Baker was the man for the job.

Already busy with India Gate and the viceroy's residence, Lutyens put Baker in charge of designing the Secretariat Buildings. It was then that the two fell out; Lutyens had planned for the viceroy's house to be built at a higher level than the Secretariat Buildings, and thus visible from a greater distance. Baker disagreed, and the ensuing argument over the gradient of the slope approaching both sets of buildings, and thus the point at which the viceroy's house comes into view, was to run and run. Baker eventually won the argument but neither man spoke to the other for years afterwards.

Connaught Place

New Delhi's religious diversity is reflected in its eclectic array of temples, mosques and churches. One of the more interesting is **Gurudwara Bangla Sahib**, the principal Sikh temple in Delhi, located southwest of Connaught Place, past all the state emporia on Baba Kharak Singh Marg. Reminiscent of Amritsar's Golden Temple – although without the actual gold – Gurudwara Bangla Sahib is dominated by a large central pool, in the middle of which lies the temple itself. Round-the-clock recitals of the Granth Sahib, the faith's holy book, lend a special atmosphere. Simple meals, served three times a day, are free to all visitors, although you may be asked to help out in the kitchen! Remove your shoes prior to entry, and cover your head – scarves are provided for those without suitable attire.

Just across the road from Gurudwara Bangla Sahib, on the roundabout where Baba Kharak Singh Marg meets Ashoka Road, stands Henry Medd's **Sacred Heart Cathedral**. The city's principal Catholic place of worship, its painted, cake-icing exterior is well maintained, as is the more austere interior. St Francis looks down from the rooftop.

West of Connaught Place, on Mandir Marg, lies the eye-catching **Lakshmi Narayan Mandir** (daily 4am–1.30pm and 2.30–9pm; free), usually referred to as the Birla Mandir after industrialist Raja Baldeo Das Birla, who financed its construction in 1938. This is one of the most colourful Hindu temples in Delhi, with a fanciful red-and-cream dome and a large shrine to Lakshmi, the goddess of wealth.

India Gate

Reminiscent of Paris's Arc de Triomphe, **India Gate** 9 was built by Lutyens in honour of soldiers who died overseas in World War I and the Afghan War of 1919. Built of cream sandstone, 42m (139ft) high, it is inscribed with the names of thousands of Indian and British soldiers, missing presumed dead. An eternal flame burns beneath the arch in memory of those who died in the 1971 war with Pakistan.

Just beyond India Gate, framed within its 9-m (30-ft) arch, stands a stone canopy, the last imperial monument to be built by Lutyens, after the death of King George V in 1936. Under the canopy he placed a marble statue of King George in imperial robes, crown and orb. The space has been empty since the statue was moved to the Coronation Memorial site after independence (see page 37).

Lakshmi Narayan Mandir temple

Encircling the India Gate road intersection sit the residences built by Lutyens for the rulers of Indian princely states. The relative importance of a state was at that time denoted by the number of guns used by the British to salute its leader. Hyderabad, Jaipur, Baroda and Bikaner were the only ones afforded the full 21 guns, a status reflected in the elaborate nature of the palaces built for their leaders. Perhaps the most impressive of them is

Hyderabad House, now used as the State Guest House for foreign dignitaries. **Baroda House** is now part of the headquarters of the Northern Railway, while **Bikaner House** is home to the Rajasthan Tourist Board.

Rajpath

India Gate forms the centrepiece of what is effectively a large roundabout, with roads leading away from it like a starburst. The most majestic of these boulevards is **Rajpath ⑩**, a wide, arrow-straight avenue flanked by lawns and water pools on either side, which runs west, climbing a gentle hill between the two **Secretariat Buildings ⑪**, designed by Herbert Baker in a style strikingly similar to the government buildings he created in Pretoria. Today they are home to the Ministries of Home, Finance and Foreign Affairs, their classical façades and grandiose proportions lending an air of imposing authority, particularly dramatic at sunset.

At the top of the hill stands the monumental **Rashtrapati Bhawan**, originally the viceroy's residence, and now the official home of the president of India. The centrepiece of Lutyens' New Delhi, this imposing domed structure – built in a rather austere classical style enlivened with discrete Indian decorative touches – is one of the grandest Raj-era buildings in the country, though unfortunately it's not open to the public. The best you can do is admire it from the top of Rajpath, although its gardens are open to visitors in February, allowing a slightly closer look.

Display at the National Museum

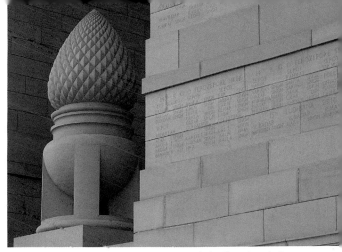

India Gate inscriptions

To the northeast of the Secretariat Buildings is **Sansad Bhawan**, now home to the Indian Houses of Parliament. Designed by Baker, the building is circular in shape and classical in appearance, the overall effect reminiscent of ancient Rome. West of Sansad Bhawan is the Church of the Redemption, whose slightly unprepossessing exterior belies the beautiful interior within.

National Museum

The **National Museum** ⑫ (Tue–Sun 10am–5pm; charge; www.nationalmuseumindia.gov.in), on Janpath just south of Rajpath, houses India's foremost collection of Asian antiquities. While not especially well displayed, the collection has some fascinating items which are must-sees for anyone with an interest in ancient civilisations.

The ground-floor exhibits are mostly prehistoric, including toys, jewellery and sculpture from the Harappan civilisation

(2400–1500BC) and the much-photographed statuette of a dancing girl found at Moenjo Daro in present-day Pakistan. Also on this floor are Gupta terracottas, including a bust of Vishnu recovered from a temple near Lal Kot, Delhi's first city, early South Indian sculpture and a collection of Buddhist bronzes.

Highlights on the first floor include an outstanding collection of miniature paintings, beautifully illustrated manuscripts, memoirs written by the Moghul emperor Jehangir and Central Asian antiquities discovered by the British archaeologist Aurel Stein. The second floor houses an eclectic range of weapons, musical instruments and tribal art.

National Gallery of Modern Art

Housed in the impressive surroundings of what was the maharaja of Jaipur's Delhi residence, just to the southeast of India Gate, the **National Gallery of Modern Art** (Tue–Sun 10am–5pm; free) comprises a huge collection of both Indian and international art. The ground floor is dedicated to post-1930 exhibits; to see the earliest work first, start on the first floor. India's best-known modern artists,

Rashtrapati Bhawan gate detail

including Amrita Shergil, Rabindranath Tagore and Nandalal Bose, are well represented. Most of the works by foreign artists were created during visits to India.

Crafts Museum

Part of the **Pragati Maidan** complex, Delhi's foremost exhibition centre, east of India Gate on Mathura Road but entered from Bhairon

Inside the National Gallery of Modern Art

Marg, the **Crafts Museum** ⓲ (Tue–Sun 10am–5pm; free) displays handicrafts from all over India. Particularly impressive are two large collections of textiles and costumes; the Kashmiri needlework and embroidery are exceptionally detailed. Also on display are some excellent examples of woodwork and metalwork. In addition, the museum features live displays of how the various crafts are made, and has as an outdoor area containing mock-ups of the different types of dwellings found in rural India.

Purana Qila

Immediately south of the Crafts Museum lies the sixth city of Delhi, **Purana Qila** ⓮ (Old Fort; daily sunrise–sunset; charge), begun by Humayun, the second Moghul emperor, and finished by his great rival, the Afghan Sher Shah. Built on what is thought to be the site of the city of Indraprastha, mentioned in the Mahabharata epic, the fort is surrounded by massive walls. Most of the interior is now parkland, although two fine buildings remain: the **Qila-i-Kuhna Masjid**, built by Sher Shah in 1541 in the Afghan style, and the unusual, octagonal Sher Mandal library-cum-observatory, where Humayun died after falling down a flight of steep stone steps (see page 18).

Gandhi Memorials

At 5 Tees Jan Marg, close to Claridges Hotel, due south of the National Museum, **Gandhi Smriti** ⑮ (Tue–Sun 10am–5pm; free; http://gandhismriti.nic.in) occupies the house where Mahatma Gandhi was shot in 1948. The possessions he had with him at the house are still there, as well as photos and other memorabilia – a more intimate and touching memorial to the great man than the Gandhi Memorial Museum at Raj Ghat (see page 38).

Indira Gandhi was shot dead in the gardens of her house at 1 Safdarjang Road, just west of Gandhi Smriti, by two of her Sikh bodyguards in 1984. The house has since been converted into the **Indira Gandhi Memorial Museum** (Tue–Sun 9.30am–5pm; free), which contains many of her personal belongings, including the sari she was wearing on the day she was shot. A recording of her voice is relayed throughout the

Purana Qila

house, and soldiers guard the still blood-stained spot where she fell.

West of the Indira Gandhi Museum is **Teen Murti Bhawan**, formerly known as Flagstaff House, which was the official residence of the first prime minister of India, Jawaharlal Nehru, from 1948 until his death in 1964. It has since been converted into the **Nehru National Museum**  (Tue–Sun 9am–5.30pm; free), with many of the rooms left exactly as he kept them, and a range of exhibits which make a good introduction to the independence movement. The **Nehru Planetarium** (charge) in the same grounds has shows in English at 11.30am and 3pm.

Moving west again from here, at the junction of Willingdon Crescent and Sardar Patel Marg, stands an impressive bronze sculpture commemorating the famous **Dandi March** ⓱, orchestrated by Mahatma Gandhi in 1931 against oppressive salt taxes imposed by the colonial regime.

National Rail Museum

Further to the south is the **National Rail Museum** ⓲ (daily Apr–Sept 9.30am–1pm and 1.30–7.30pm; Oct–Mar 9.30am–1pm and 1.30–5.30pm; charge). This large collection of all things locomotive appeals to rail buffs young and old. Situated off Nyaya Marg in Chanakyapuri, it has a massive array of machinery, much of it steam-powered. There are also some of the luxury carriages used by maharajas and visiting dignitaries, push-button exhibits and other child-friendly attractions including a toy train ride.

Dandi March Memorial

Lodi Gardens

LODI GARDENS AND NIZAMUDDIN

The suburbs south of New Delhi are now home to some of the capital's most desirable residential districts, although the area's largely modern appearance belies its long history and absorbing roster of attractions. It was here that the settlement of Delhi was originally established, and where many of the city's former rulers lived and died: their deeds are commemorated in the palaces, forts and tombs scattered throughout the area, particularly between the sylvan Lodi Gardens and the atmospheric Muslim dargah (tomb) at Nizamuddin.

Humayun's Tomb

One of the best-preserved Moghul monuments in India, **Humayun's Tomb** ⑲ anticipates many of the architectural features of the later Taj Mahal, and very nearly achieves the same elegance and grace. The complex, built in 1570, is actually home to a large number of tombs, including those of many royal family members, as well as Humayun's barber. Its construction was supervised by Humayun's second wife, Haji Begum, who camped on site throughout the nine-year project.

On entering the complex, you'll notice a stone gateway leading through the wall on the right. Through this lies the unrestored, but evocative, **Isa Khan's Tomb**. Parts of the original tilework remain, giving an insight into how the building must have originally looked.

Coming back through the gateway, turn right and the second archway will lead you into the formal gardens surrounding the main tomb. These are laid out in the traditional *charbagh* design, divided by water channels into four separate areas – those at the Taj Mahal follow the same pattern. The three high walls that enclose the garden are testimony to the changing course of the Yamuna River, which originally

Humayun's Tomb

ran directly past the tomb
and would have formed the
fourth boundary.

The main mausoleum sits
on a red-sandstone platform,
its facade dominated by a
huge central arch which was
to become a standard fea-
ture of subsequent Moghul
tombs. The small arches lining the platform lead to the
tombs of lesser royals. The
building itself, also of red

Nizamuddin's Shrine

sandstone, is inlaid with black-and-white marble and has at
its centre the octagonal chamber containing the tomb of
Humayun himself, as well as those of other Moghul dignitaries. The 38-m (125-ft) high dome was the first of its type in
India; domes had until then been simple hemispheres rather
than the fuller onion shape seen here.

Nizamuddin

Across busy Mathura Road, nestled in the narrow alleyways of Nizamuddin village, is **Nizamuddin Dargah ❹**,
the tomb and shrine of one of Sufism's most revered saints,
Shaikh Hazrat Nizamuddin Aulia Chisti (1236–1325). He was
hugely popular during his lifetime, and the shrine remains an
important Sufi pilgrimage site, while the sheikh's doctrine
of religious tolerance means that adherents of many faiths
come here too.

The shrine sits in the centre of a marble courtyard, sur-
rounded by a mosque and an assortment of other tombs.
While Nizamuddin's mausoleum dates from the time of the
holy man's death in 1325 aged 92, the elegant pavilion that
covers it was a later addition by Shah Jahan. A particularly

good time to visit is towards sunset, when musicians gather around the tomb to perform *qawwalis* in honour of this mystic saint – Thursdays attract particularly large crowds.

Men and children visiting the shrine should not miss out on the chance to have their legs and feet massaged. This service is offered on the streetside by nimble-fingered men, and as such is not available to women (who tend to have masseurs visit them in their homes). A wide range of natural oils are on offer, including coconut, *amla* (Indian gooseberry), *chameli* (jasmine), *sarsan* (mustard, particularly recommended as a body oil and much loved by Indian wrestlers) and *navrattan* (a mixture of nine different oils), the last two being the most commonly requested.

To the south of Humayun's Tomb, just off the main Mathura Road in an area known as Nizamuddin East, lies the tomb of **Abdur Rahim Khan**, son of Akbar's most loyal protector in his early years, who carried the title of Khan-i-Khanan. He was later remembered chiefly for his poetry, which is still popular in India today. His tomb was designed along

Akshardham

A more recent addition to Delhi's collection of temples is Akshardham (daily Apr–Sept 10am–7pm; Oct–Mar 9am–6pm; free; www.akshardham.com), a spectacular complex inaugurated in 2005. Described as 'an enlightening journey through India's glorious art, values and contributions for the progress, happiness and harmony of mankind', it's a hugely impressive undertaking, with no expense spared in its construction. As well as some exquisite temple architecture, there are also several award-winning multimedia presentations, musical fountains and a boating lake. It's located on the eastern bank of the Yamuna River, just underneath Nizamuddin Bridge – consult the website for details.

the lines of Humayun's, and originally had a marble dome, but this was removed to be used on Safdarjung's Tomb (see page 56).

Lodi Gardens

West along Lodi Road from Nizamuddin are **Lodi Gardens** ㉑ (daily 5am–8pm; free), South Delhi's most manicured park and home to several well-preserved tombs in the Lodi style. The tomb in the southwest corner of the park belongs to Delhi sultan Muhammad Shah and dates back to 1450; its octagonal design subsequently inspired aspects of the interior layout of Humayun's Tomb and eventually the Taj Mahal.

The Muhammed Shah tomb in Lodi Gardens

Some 300m (980ft) northeast of here, near the centre of the gardens, is the sturdy **Bara Gumbad**, topped with an imposing hemispherical dome. Just north of here, the similar Shish Gumbad preserves a few of the blue tiles which would originally have decorated its dome. Another 250m (820ft) north is a fourth tomb, of Sikandar Lodi, built on a similar octagonal plan to the tomb of Muhammad Shah.

Throngs of Delhiites gather for their morning walk in Lodi Gardens. It's an excellent escape from the bustle of the city at any time of the day, however, and the garden restaurant makes for a particularly pleasant retreat (see page 112).

India Habitat Centre

Diagonally opposite Lodi Gardens is the curiously named **India Habitat Centre** (www.indiahabitat.org). This sprawling cultural complex contains a number of different galleries, theatres and restaurants, including an American-style diner and a multi-cuisine food court which would not look out of place in a Western shopping mall. It's always worth dropping in to see what's happening; the art and photography exhibitions are of a consistently high standard.

At the mid-point of Lodi Road you'll find **Tibet House** (Mon–Fri 10am–5.30pm; free). This small museum has an excellent collection of Tibetan artefacts as well as information about the struggle for the freedom of Tibet. There's also a library and a shop selling Tibetan handicrafts.

Safdarjung's Tomb

At the far western end of Lodi Road is **Safdarjung's Tomb** ㉒ (daily sunrise–sunset; charge), the mausoleum of Safdarjung, *wazir* (chief minister) of the Moghul emperor Muhammad Shah. Finished in 1774, this was the very last of India's great Moghul garden tombs, and is often compared, always unfavourably, with Humayun's and the Taj Mahal, which it somewhat resembles – although the mausoleum's peaceful garden setting and delicately decorated red-sandstone facades have their own distinctive form.

SOUTH DELHI

Beyond the flyover by Sardarjung Airport lies South Delhi proper. Many of Delhi's most desirable residential areas are located here, the affluence of the inhabitants reflected in both the extravagant architecture of some of the houses, no two of which are alike, and the services and facilities on offer, unmatched in any other part of town. In the very south of the city are the impressive remains of the Qutb Minar, Tughlaqabad and Mehrauli, as well as Delhi's biggest temple complexes.

Dilli Haat and INA Market

Midway between Safdarjung's Tomb and Hauz Khas Village stand these two wildly contrasting markets, facing each other on opposite sides of the main road, Aurobindo Marg. **Dilli Haat** is a Delhi Tourism enterprise, where a small entrance fee is charged to enter a pleasant complex of crafts stalls and eateries offering cuisine from all over India. Events are held throughout the year, with the Dastkar festival in November always hugely popular with tourists and locals alike.

INA (Indian National Army; Tue–Sun), on the other hand, is a sprawling market famed for its fruit, vegetables, meat and fish. It is not for the faint-hearted; the poultry, for example, is kept alive until the moment you order it, lending the whole establishment a pungent aroma.

Hauz Khas

Just as you come into **Hauz Khas Village** ㉓, you'll notice the entrance to the 'Deer Park' on your right-hand side. Believe it or not, this really is home to a herd of deer, similar in appearance to those that populate London's Richmond Park. Their diet is markedly different, however; a popular pastime involves buying a mala, or garland, of marigolds from the stall opposite the temple on the road that leads to Hauz Khas Village, and then unstringing them and throwing them through the fence to the flower-devouring deer.

Directly to the south lie the last surviving remains of Delhi's second city at **Hauz Khas** (Royal Tank). The area takes its name from the reservoir created by Ala-ud-din Khalji in 1300 to provide water for his new city of Siri *(see below)*. Fifty years later Feroz Shah Tughlaq repaired the tank and founded a *madarsa* (college) by the side of the reservoir, as well as

INA Market

creating an enclosure for his own tomb.

A kilometre (just over 0.5 mile) due east, the few last remains of the outer walls of Ala-ud-din Khalji's city of **Siri** can be made out in the undergrowth off Khel Gaon Marg. The fort was purpose-built to try to defend Ala-ud-din and his people from attacks by marauding Mongols, who were fond of

Ancient archways at Hauz Khaz

invading Delhi and in 1298 managed to ransack the city's suburbs. So unchallenged did they feel that a large number of Mongols chose to stay on in Delhi once the attack was over, a mistake they would live to regret. Having been forced to retreat as far back as the area around the Qutb Minar, Ala-ud-din went on a rampage of his own once the coast

Lal dora

South Delhi is dotted with seemingly chaotic quarters of unplanned development. When the British were deciding revenue conditions, it was decreed that special compensation should be given to village areas, which were outlined on a map with a red pen, and hence came to be known as *lal dora*, or red border, villages. Over the years these areas have continued to benefit from less stringent government control, with land-use and property-tax restrictions much less severe than in other areas. Having been in existence for some time, these areas generally have one or two historical monuments secreted somewhere amid the mayhem, making them fascinating areas to wander around; Hauz Khas Village is a particularly good example.

was clear. Every remaining Mongol was murdered, their severed heads first put on public display and then incorporated into the walls of Siri Fort, the building of which had just begun. Whereas most of Delhi's cities were named after their founder, Siri is derived from the Hindi word *sir*, meaning 'head'.

Baha'i Temple

The remarkable white-marble **Baha'i Temple** ㉔ (Apr–Sept Tue–Sun 9am–7pm; Oct–Mar Tue–Sun 9.30am–5.30pm; free), completed in 1981, is widely known as the Lotus Temple because of its shape. Forty-five lotus petals form the walls. Internally this gives a wonderful impression of light and space, helped by the 34-m (112-ft) high ceiling. There are audio-visual presentations on the Baha'i faith roughly every two hours, and the temple is open to visitors of every

The Baha'i Temple

religion. Seen from a distance, the exterior looks particularly striking by night, when floodlights help give the impression of the temple floating on water. It is situated close to Nehru Place, to the southeast of Delhi.

Kalkaji Temple

Just to the south of the Baha'i Temple, accessed from the main Outer Ring Road, stands

Kalkaji Temple

Kalkaji Temple (or *mandir*). A Hindu temple dedicated to the goddess Kalka Devi, it was founded as early as 1764, when a farmer is said to have built the temple in honour of a cow that gave all its milk to the goddess. Additions were made during the 19th century, but most parts of the domed, 12-sided building are modern. Relatively unadorned, this temple makes an interesting contrast to its flashier Baha'i neighbour, and comes alive particularly during the festival of Navaratri in October, when thousands of pilgrims flock here.

Tughlaqabad

Due south of the Baha'i Temple stand the massive walls of **Tughlaqabad** ❷⑤ (sunrise–sunset; charge), the third city of Delhi, built by the first of the Tughlaq rulers, Ghiyas-ud-din Tughlaq, in the 1320s. Houses, palaces and temples once stood here; today, it is the city walls, 6km (4 miles) in circumference, that are most prominent, and give the best impression of the scale of this vast settlement. Muhammad-bin-Tughlaq succeeded his father five years after the completion of the city, but in true Tughlaq fashion decided that he had to build a capital of his own, and moved everyone

The iron pillar at the Qutb Minar

out, so Tughlaqabad was occupied for a far shorter period of time than it took to build.

On the opposite side of the Mehrauli–Badarpur Road to the south of the walled city stands Ghiyas-ud-din Tughlaq's **tomb**, originally in the centre of a lake (now dry) and connected via a causeway. The high esteem in which the city's founder was held is reflected in the use of sandstone to build his final resting place, rather than the cheaper local stone used elsewhere.

Qutb Minar complex

About 7km (4.5 miles) due west of Tughlaqabad, the **Qutb Minar** ㉖ (sunrise–sunset; charge) and its surrounding buildings were the first major Islamic constructions in India and mark the centre of the Slave dynasty's rule over Delhi.

The Qutb Minar itself was built by Qutb-ud-din Aibak, the Turkish slave-general appointed governor of Delhi by Muhammad of Ghor, who later reigned as sultan. Its construction followed the near obliteration by Muhammad's troops of all religious monuments on the North Indian plain, be they Hindu, Buddhist or Jain, and was intended to celebrate the victory of Islam over the infidels. Qutb-ud-din started work in 1199, but could only complete the base before his death in 1210. His son-in-law, Iltutmish, succeeded him and added a further three storeys.

After twice sustaining lightning damage during the 1300s, the tower was renovated by Feroz Shah Tughlaq, who also added a fifth storey topped by an ornate cupola. An earthquake in 1803 toppled the cupola, however,

and it was replaced in 1829 by another built by Major Robert Smith. Not quite as elegant as the original, the British engineer's handiwork was removed in 1848 and now lies in the adjacent gardens. The tower today stands 73m (240ft) high, tapering in diameter from 14m (46ft) at the base to just 2.5m (8ft) at the top.

Next to the tower stands India's first mosque, **Quwwat-ul-Islam (Might of Islam) Masjid**. Started by Qutb-ud-din in 1192, the original mosque was built from the remains of 27 Hindu and Jain temples, a fact evinced by the panoply of styles within. Of particular note is the sandstone screen which forms the mosque's facade, originally Indo-Islamic in style but with more purely Islamic later additions, reflecting the growing confidence of India's rapidly expanding Muslim population.

Iltutmish extended the mosque in response to Islam's increasing popularity, incorporating as he did so the Qutb Minar within the boundary walls, and thus producing the first example of a mosque with integral minaret, a design since adopted by mosques the world over. **Iltutmish's Tomb** lies to the west of the mosque, the earliest surviving example of an Indian ruler's tomb, Hindus having been long-time practitioners of cremation. The quality of the interior carving is particularly fine. The tomb is thought to have

Garden of the Five Senses

been originally covered by a dome which has since collapsed, fragments of which can be seen lying around the building.

Mehrauli

As the site of Lal Kot, Delhi's first city, **Mehrauli** ㉗ – the area surrounding the Qutb Minar complex – is the oldest inhabited district of Delhi, a fact reflected in the myriad monuments dotted throughout its narrow lanes – though they're much less visited than the Mehrauli's popular bazaar, which sells everything from fluorescent bras to hookahs. Principal among the archaeological remains are **Bhulbhulaiyan**, the octagonal tomb of Adham Khan, a general of the Moghul emperor Akbar, built on the remains of Lal Kot's ramparts and affording good views over this ancient citadel. An Englishman named Blake converted the tomb into his residence in the 1830s; his insensitivity in removing the tomb itself to make way for his dining table is said to have led to his sudden demise soon after. Other attractions include the shrine of the Sufi saint **Qutb ud-din Bakhtiyar Kaki**, comparable but inferior to that of Nizamuddin (see page 53), and open only to men, and **Hauz-i-Shamsi**, a reservoir at the southern end of Mehrauli built by Iltutmish in 1230, which has the architecturally interesting Jahaz Mahal, a Lodi palace, on its banks.

The Garden of Five Senses

About 3km (2 miles) south of the Qutb Minar, signposted off the main Mehrauli–Gurgaon Road, lies Delhi Tourism's latest attraction, the **Garden of Five Senses** . Designed to 'stimulate one's sensory response to the environment', it's a well-thought-out 8-hectare (20-acre) site which features not only beautiful gardens but also some interesting sculpture and a solar energy park, where solar-powered bicycles are available to hire. There is also an untouched area of barren, rocky outcrops which affords good views over the city, and a handful of chic, over-priced cafés and restaurants.

Chattarpur

Visitors keen on temple architecture might like to visit **Chattarpur** ㉔, an area dotted with temples, chief among them Chattarpur Mandir itself. Built from white marble and intricately carved in the South Indian style, this Hindu structure has smaller temples within dedicated to Lords Shiva, Ganesha and Rama, but has the Goddess Durga as

Chattarpur temple complex

Rush hour traffic at Gurgaon

the chief presiding deity. One of the largest Hindu temples in Delhi, it is particularly animated during the festival of Navratri.

Continuing south from Chattarpur you'll come across the **Sanskriti Museums of Everyday Art, Indian Terracotta and Textiles** (Tue–Sat 10am–5pm; free; www.sanskriti foundation.org) on the right-hand side of the road shortly before Gurgaon. The Everyday Art collection includes objects such as jars, boxes, mirrors, toys and kitchen utensils, all entirely functional but exceptionally finely made. The display of Indian terracotta includes mythological figures, animals, decorative tiles and clay pots, again all superbly put together.

These museums are part of the Sanskriti Foundation, a non-profit organisation which aims to nurture artistic talent and thus help to preserve India's cultural heritage. This complex, known as 'Kendra', houses artists' residences, workshops, studios and galleries in addition to the two museums. The curators are keen for museum visitors to interact with the resident artists, often a fascinating experience for both parties.

OUTSKIRTS

Gurgaon and NOIDA

Delhi's most modern development, the satellite city of **Gurgaon** lies 30km (19 miles) south of the centre. An ambitious new boom town connected with an eight-lane expressway, its ultra-modern office towers, shopping malls and multiplexes offer a surreal contrast to the unplanned mayhem which characterizes much of Delhi.

Similar in concept, although somewhat more chaotic in practice, **NOIDA** (New Okhla Industrial Development Area), another satellite town, lies on the east side of the Yamuna River, so officially is in Delhi's neighbouring state, Uttar Pradesh. Gurgaon is likewise not within Delhi's jurisdiction, but in Haryana, and this partly explains the secret of the success of these two areas; Delhi's land use and tax laws are far stricter than those of the surrounding states.

Sulabh International Museum of Toilets

Located at Sulabh Gram, Mahavir Enclave, Palam-Dabri Marg in West Delhi, the **Sulabh Toilets Museum** (Mon–Sat 10.30am–5.30pm; free; www.sulabhtoiletmuseum.org) is a quirky one-off: an exhibition celebrating all things lavatorial. The use of toilets and the etiquette that goes with them is examined as far back as the Harappan civilisation (2400–1500BC), with some interesting insights into the toilet manners of mankind since. One example that stands out is that of the French monarch who chose to eat in private but use the toilet in public.

Open since 1994, the museum is part of a larger social services initiative aimed at promoting public health and hygiene across India. Uttam Nagar East Metro station is only a short walk away.

EXCURSIONS

Some of India's most memorable sights lie within easy reach of Delhi. Foremost amongst these are the great Moghul monuments of Agra and Fatehpur Sikri, while the beautiful Keoladeo Ghana National Park at Bharatpur, just over an hour's drive from Agra, provides a restful rural contrast to the helter-skelter capital. Further afield, the magnificent Golden Temple in Amritsar can also be reached on an overnight trip from Delhi.

Agra
Taj Mahal
The world's most beautiful building and greatest monument to love, the **Taj Mahal** (Sat–Thur 6am–7pm; charge) lies just two-and-a-half hours from Delhi by express train. However

The incomparable Taj Mahal

many pictures you've seen of it, nothing prepares you for the sublime reality, and if you're anywhere near Delhi, you'd be mad to miss it.

Shah Jahan, the Moghul emperor responsible for making Delhi the capital of Moghul India, and builder of the Red Fort and Jama Masjid, was so grief-stricken by the death of his wife,

The Taj by night

Aficionados maintain the Taj is at its most ethereal in the light of a full moon, which is why the Archeological Survey of India open the complex for five nights each month during the full-moon period. You'll need to buy a ticket the day before from the ASI office at 22 Mall Road (0562/222 7261).

Mumtaz Mahal, in 1631, that he resolved to build her a resting place which in its exquisite beauty would reflect the magnitude of his love for her. The Taj Mahal was the extraordinary result, taking 20,000 workers 22 years to build, at an estimated cost of US$500 million in today's terms.

Sadly, the end of the story was no happier than the beginning; when Shah Jahan's son, Aurangzeb, came to the throne, he locked his father in Agra Fort and threw away the key. Shah Jahan spent his last eight years imprisoned, his only view was that of his wife's mausoleum, at which he reputedly gazed longingly until his dying day.

Although the quality of the white marble used in the construction of the Taj is such that it seems to radiate light at any time of day, the effect at sunrise and sunset is particularly striking. It's worth noting that if you've already been inside and would like to see the Taj from another angle, the view from the other side of the river is equally stunning, although it does involve a rickshaw ride as the nearest bridge is a kilometre or two (about 1 mile) from the Taj – ask for Mehtab Bagh.

You can approach the Taj Mahal from either the eastern or western **entrances**. Take as little as possible with you as there's

a stringent security check on entry and there's a whole range of items you're not allowed to take in, including phones, food, drink, cigarettes and tripods. You may well have seen the outline of the Taj from a distance before you actually go in, but once you're inside the first courtyard, the whole building is obscured from view by the massive **gateway**. This is a deliberate ploy, reminding the visitor that they are about to enter a different world, the gateway serving as a divide between the secular world and paradise.

Exquisite inlay work at the Taj Mahal

Even as you stand beneath the gateway's massive arch (the brass doors are a recent addition; the originals were solid silver but were plundered by the Jats) still only the tomb itself is visible. As you walk through the archway, the dome and then the minarets come gradually into view, until finally the whole magnificent structure is unveiled. Although the gardens are well maintained, they're not a patch on how they would have originally looked, with all the watercourses in full flow, stocked with fish, and the trees full of exotic birds, perhaps the ultimate example of the Persian *charbagh* design. Take time to wander through the avenues to either side of the busy central causeway: they're a good place to enjoy uninterrupted views of the Taj, and to contemplate its perfection from a different angle.

The tomb itself is flanked by two identical sandstone buildings; the one to the left, or west, is a **mosque**, while the other,
known as the **jawab**, is there simply to maintain the symme-
try of the site. On approaching the tomb itself, notice how
the minarets lean away from the building, a deliberate slant
intended to ensure they would fall away from the tomb in
the event of an earthquake. Shoes must be removed before
climbing the steps to the tomb; if you're wearing socks, leave
them on – white marble can get scorchingly hot – otherwise
overshoes are available to rent.

The exterior of the tomb is beautifully inlaid, using a technique known as *pietra dura*, lesser examples of which you'll
see for sale in Agra. The **interior** of the tomb has further
examples of this work, including the marble screen around
the central tomb itself. Carved from one huge block of
marble, the screen was commissioned by Aurangzeb, who
removed the silver original for fear of it being stolen. The
lamp which originally hung above the tomb was stolen, however; this one was donated by the viceroy Lord Curzon in
1899. Shah Jahan's tomb is the larger one to the side of that
of Mumtaz, the only asymmetrical feature in the Taj Mahal,
having been placed there by Aurangzeb against the dictates
of the original plan.

Agra Fort

Often overshadowed by the Taj Mahal, **Agra Fort** (daily
sunrise–sunset; charge, cheaper when combined with Taj
Mahal ticket) is an exceptional building in its own right,
and has been better preserved and respected than Delhi's
Red Fort. Construction of the fort was begun by Akbar in
1565, although the whole complex was significantly embel-
lished and expanded by his grandson, Shah Jahan. Entrance
is via the massive Amar Singh gate on the fort's southern
perimeter.

Diwan-i-Am in Agra Fort

The first building you come across is **Jehangir Palace,** the only significant building to survive from Akbar's original fort. Encompassing an interesting blend of Hindu and Persian styles, it is thought to have been used as living quarters for some of Akbar's most important wives; the large stone bowl in front of the building would have been used for bathing.

As you continue into the palace complex built by Shah Jahan, his private palace is the first structure you'll see, built using his favoured white marble; together with the highly decorated, octagonal **Mussaman Burj** tower, which is also visible, this is where the emperor spent the last eight years of his life. Immediately in front are the **Anguri Bagh** formal gardens, featuring a beautifully textured waterslide set into the marble wall.

The other side of the tower is the **Shish Mahal** (Mirror Palace), which would have originally had both its walls and ceiling inset with tiny mirrors. Next is the **Diwan-i-Khas**

(Hall of Private Audiences), a luxurious chamber into which only the highest-ranking dignitaries would have been allowed. From here, an internal staircase leads to the **Diwan-i-Am** (Hall of Public Audiences), where the emperor would have met his subjects, passing judgement on the people's grievances. The alcove at the back was originally designed to house the famous Peacock Throne, taken from here to Delhi's Red Fort by Shah Jahan, and then carried off to Tehran by Nadir Shah in 1739 (see page 20).

The domes of the **Moti Masjid** (Pearl Mosque) are visible from the Diwan-i-Am, but the building itself is structurally unsound and so cannot be entered. However, the **Nangina Masjid** (Gem Mosque), used by the ladies of the court, is open, and well worth visiting.

I'timad-ud-Daulah

Also known as the 'baby Taj', the **I'timad-ud-Daulah** (sunrise–sunset; charge) was in some ways a precursor to its more illustrious namesake. It was the first building to be entirely faced with white marble and decorated with semi-precious stones, the technique known as *pietra dura* which was also used on the Taj Mahal. It's located on the opposite side of the Yamuna River to the Taj Mahal and Agra Fort.

Significantly, this charming mausoleum was built by a woman, Nur Jahan, who commissioned it for her father, Ghiyas Beg, Jehangir's wazir (chief minister). She subsequently became Jehangir's wife, and is thought to have alluded to her husband's fondness for alcohol, of which she did not altogether approve, in the many wine-jug motifs which adorn the tomb's exquisite exterior.

Fatehpur Sikri

About 40km (25 miles) west of Agra, **Fatehpur Sikri** is made up of two halves, the small, relatively modern town and,

The exterior of the I'timad-ud-Daulah

above it, the magnificent remains of the city built by Akbar but largely abandoned just a few years after its completion in 1585. While there is some accommodation in the town, most people choose to visit from either Agra or Bharatpur.

The story goes that Akbar, at 26 years old, and having already been in power for 13 years, had but one overriding concern. His position as ruler of Hindustan was well consolidated, his even-handed treatment of the Hindus having earned him the love and respect of his people. However, there was no heir to this great empire he'd so painstakingly put together, and the thought of it all falling apart after his death was too much for him to bear.

He began to seek the counsel of holy men wherever he went; he had a prodigious array of wives, but all the children hitherto born to him had died in infancy, and he wanted to know why. One such man he visited was Sheikh Salim Chisti, who lived in the small village of Sikri. The holy man told the emperor that he would have three sons. Soon after, one of the emperor's wives fell pregnant, prompting the proud father to send her to Sikri to be close to this talismanic sage during her pregnancy. A son was indeed born, later to become Jehangir, and was followed in short order by two more boys.

Akbar couldn't believe his luck, and felt so indebted to Salim Chisti that he resolved to build a whole new city next to the village of Sikri, to become his new capital. Fourteen years in the making, Fatehpur (victory) Sikri was Akbar's most ambitious project by far, and aimed to reflect the great leader's multi-faith spirituality. Although now seen as one of the great legacies of Moghul rule, it became known as Akbar's greatest folly when he upped sticks and left after living there for just four years. The precise reasons for his departure remain unclear; the erratic water supply is often thought to have been a factor, as are the political ramifications of Akbar having based himself so far from the major cities of his empire.

Sikandra

Another monumental Moghul tomb, Akbar's mausoleum (sunrise–sunset; charge) at Sikandra, 10km (6 miles) north of Agra, is best visited either on the way in or out of Agra by road. The site's imposing gateway reflects the high esteem in which Akbar was held; he was regarded by many as the greatest and most compassionate of the Moghul emperors. Beyond the gateway lie beautifully maintained gardens, extraordinarily serene given their close proximity to the main Agra–Delhi highway. Spotted deer roam free, while tame and tourist-inured monkeys approach inquisitively along the broad central path leading to the imposing red-sandstone mausoleum itself, its facades attractively inlaid with white marble. A narrow passageway leads down to a subterranean crypt, where you'll find Akbar's simple tomb.

Fatehpur Sikri

Effectively empty since the early 1600s, the whole complex is fantastically well preserved, testimony to both the durability of the local sandstone and the high quality of the workmanship. The main sights are split into two distinct areas, the Jama Masjid (sunrise–sunset; free) and the Royal Palace complex (sunrise–sunset; charge). You are likely to be inundated by guides offering their services; this is one place where a good guide can be indispensable, as there's not much in the way of information on the way round. But make sure you get one of the official guides – if in doubt, check at the ticket office. Note that there are two of these. The busiest is next to the Jodh Bai entrance, next to the main car park, while the second, far less crowded entrance can be accessed by taking the right fork as soon as you enter Fatehpur Sikri from the direction of Agra.

Jama Masjid

Even by outsized Moghul standards, the main gateway to the Jama Masjid, the Buland Darwaza, is exceptionally large and gives an impression of unequivocal authority. The courtyard into which it leads is sizeable as well, not dissimilar in terms of both size and style to the courtyard of Delhi's Jama Masjid. The undisputed highlight of this mosque, however, is the **Tomb of Sheikh Salim Chisti**, the man without whom none of this would have been here.

Constructed using white marble of only the highest quality, the tomb-cum-shrine has an almost spellbinding brilliance. The standard of the workmanship is second to none; the *jali* (latticework screens) are particularly impressive, as is the mother-of-pearl canopy over the tomb itself. Women wanting to conceive still come here in the hope of having the same experience as Akbar, petitioning the saint by tying red and orange threads to the screens.

The Royal Palace

As you enter the complex from the south, the first building you come to is the **Palace of Jodh Bai**, an elegant example of the fusing of different architectural and religious styles that continues throughout the city. Its columns are typically Hindu, topped by Islamic cupolas and blue Persian roof tiles. At the far side you'll see what look like stables; like many of Fatehpur Sikri's buildings, the precise use of these is not known for sure. While hoops suggest that animals were indeed tethered here, it is thought more likely that the buildings housed servants.

Jali screen at the Tomb of Sheikh Salim Chisti

Salim's request

'In return for your friendship and grace', said the emperor to Sheikh Salim Chisti, 'I'll protect and preserve you.' Unmoved, the Sufi replied: 'You can name your first son after me.' The following August, a son was born. He was duly named Salim (later Jehangir).

Continuing north, the next building is the **Palace of the Christian Wife**. This was home to Akbar's Goan wife, Maryam, the very lady who fell pregnant after Akbar's encounter with Salim Chisti, and bore him his first son, Jehangir. Just behind is the fanciful **Panch Mahal**, a five-storey tower with each level a little smaller than the one below, used by the ladies of the court and overlooking the **Ladies' Garden**. The 56 columns on the second floor are distinctly Hindu in design and all different to each other.

Just as you enter the main courtyard, you'll notice an outsize chequerboard set in the paving slabs. This is where Akbar used to play *Pachisi* (Twenty-Five) – an intricate game from which ludo is thought to derive – reputedly using slave girls as pieces. Heading north, you'll pass the intricately carved, Gujarati-style **Astrologer's Kiosk**, before arriving at the **Treasury**. Here the court's substantial coffers were guarded by mythical sea creatures, which still look down from the ceiling today.

Directly in front of the Treasury is the **Diwan-i-Khas** (Hall of Private Audiences), the building which perhaps more than any other epitomises the character and interests of Akbar. Although relatively plain from the outside, the interior is absolutely unique. One large space, it is dominated by a central pillar which rises up to form a circular throne platform. This is connected to the balconies which line the chamber's interior by four narrow bridges. Akbar would sit in the middle, debating with wise men of every religious persuasion surrounding him on the balconies while lesser courtiers could listen in from the ground floor. This ideal of religious synthesis can be seen in the carvings on the pillar itself; the lower section is divided into four tiers, incorporating Muslim, Hindu, Christian and Buddhist designs.

Dominating the courtyard to the eastern side is the **Diwan-i-Am** (Hall of Public Audiences), a much more traditional design, where Akbar would sit to listen to the affairs of his people, dispensing justice with his trademark fairness.

Mathura and Vrindavan

Some 50km (31 miles) north of Agra on the road to Delhi, the towns of Mathura and Vrindavan are considered two of the most sacred in India, thanks to their associations with the blue-skinned, flute-playing god Krishna, who is believed to have been born in Mathura and to have grown up in the countryside around Vrindavan.

Panch Mahal

The biggish industrial town of Mathura is home to the **Kesava Deo Mandir**, built on the very spot where Krishna was born; the Potara Kund tank, where his clothes were washed; and the numerous riverside ghats, of which **Vishram Ghat** is the best known. The much smaller and more peaceful riverside town of Vrindavan offers a pleasant respite from the hustle and bustle of Mathura, and is also worth a visit, as much to observe the many visiting pilgrims as to see the beautiful ghats.

Bird sanctuaries

On the outskirts of Bharatpur, 50km (31 miles) west from Agra, is the world-famous **Keoladeo Ghana National Park** (daily Apr–Sept 6am–6pm; Oct–Mar 6.30am–5pm; charge), one of Asia's most spectacular bird sanctuaries. Once the maharaja of Bharatpur's hunting ground, the park has been a bird sanctuary since 1957. There are plenty of good budget

Vishram Ghat

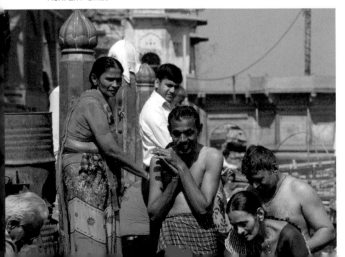

and mid-range accommodation options here, and some tourists choose to use this as their base, visiting the more hectic tourist centres of Agra and Fatehpur Sikri by day, and returning to Bharatpur's relative tranquillity by night.

Spoonbill

The park can be entered only on foot, by bicycle or cycle rickshaw, which adds greatly to the peacefulness of the environment, for the birds and visitors alike. Boat rides are another great way to go birdwatching. Guides are available at the park gate. The best time to visit is from October to March, when migratory birds land in their thousands, from egrets, storks, kingfishers and spoonbills to falcons, eagles, bee-eaters and owls. There's also plenty of other wildlife, including monkeys, deer, antelope, hyenas and wild boar.

Sadly, the repeated failure of the monsoons since 2005 has posed a major threat to this fragile eco-system– in the particularly severe drought of 2007, the entire area dried up, provoking the wholesale departure of Keoladeo's avian population, and threatening the park's all-important Unesco World Heritage Site status. However, work was begun in June 2011 on a pipeline which should secure the long-term future of this famous reserve by channelling water to it from the nearby River Chambal.

For keen ornithologists with little time on their hands, **Sultanpur Bird Sanctuary** is a more convenient option. Not far past Gurgaon, off the NH8 and 46km (29 miles) from Delhi, this small sanctuary can make a fascinating diversion, especially in the winter months when migratory birds gather

The Golden Temple at Amritsar

and there is more water in the lake. Cranes, including the sarus and demoiselle, are the biggest draw.

Amritsar

Six hours from Delhi by train, Amritsar's **Golden Temple** is a sacred site which Delhi visitors with a couple of spare days on their hands should consider visiting. The centre of the Sikh faith, it is a place endowed with an extraordinary sense of spirituality, strength and self-sufficiency. The temple itself, set in the middle of a large holy lake, looks particularly impressive at dawn, which is easily the best time to visit.

Before entering the temple, visitors should remove their shoes (free cloakrooms are available), wash their feet and cover their head with one of the scarves provided. The lilting sound of prayer recitals, which continue throughout the day and night, will greet you as you enter, as will the stunning site of the Harmandir, the Golden Temple itself.

Turn left at the bottom of the stairs; the temple should be approached in a clockwise direction. In stark contrast to the beautiful surroundings, the first things you may notice are the corrugated-iron huts which shield bathing women from view. After passing the first corner you'll see a tree at the edge of the tank, the site of a healing miracle and a particularly popular spot for bathing.

The archway to the right shortly afterwards leads to the sleeping quarters, where pilgrims are put up free of charge for three days, and to the kitchen. The whole complex has an industrious air, but nowhere more so than the kitchen. It produces up to 3,000 meals a day, offered to all visitors regardless of religion or caste. As you approach the dining hall, take a look at the white hut to the left, which houses a remarkable contraption dedicated to the production of chapattis.

The washing-up area to the right is equally impressive – the scale of the operation can be seen from the thousands of metal plates washed and ready to use. While all the food is free, visitors are encouraged to help clean the dishes, and can be seen doing so with much gusto. Returning to the main tank, you'll pass a shrine commemorating the heroic if grisly end of one Baba Deep Singh; his story is recounted next to the painting.

The temple itself is reached by a 60-m (200-ft) causeway, at the end of which sweet *prasad* is handed out to be offered in worship. The ground floor, often full of worshippers, contains the **Granth Sahib**, the holy book of the Sikh faith. It is brought here each morning before dawn from the Akal Takhat (opposite the temple) and returned there at night, a lively procedure that visitors are welcome to watch. Readings from the book are carried out continuously on the first floor; the palanquin used to transport the Granth Sahib can also be seen here.

WHAT TO DO

SHOPPING

Delhi offers a massive variety of shopping opportunities, from haggling for handicraft bargains in the back lanes of Old Delhi to choosing from the biggest international brands in huge, air-conditioned malls. There are more and more boutiques popping up, with Indian fashion designers becoming increasingly well known the world over, while jewellery has always been a great buy here, and books a lot cheaper than in the West.

Where to Buy

Jewellery. For interesting designs in silver, try Silverlines, 1st floor, 18 Babar Road, in Bengali Market east of Connaught Place, which has an absolutely vast range. The majority of their designs are not on display, so don't be afraid to keep asking to see more. Traditional and inexpensive Indian silver jewellery is available in

> ### Bargaining tips
>
> Outside of government emporia and the more exclusive shops, it is customary to bargain. The classic strategy is to offer half what is being asked by the vendor and slowly move up to about two-thirds of the original price. Don't start bargaining unless you really want the item.

Lajpat Nagar's Central Market in south Delhi, around 2km (1 mile) south of Nizamuddin; for ethnic silver, head for the silver bazaar in Gole Market, just west of Connaught Place. Sunder Nagar Market, just south of the Purana Qila, is great for all kinds of jewellery, from ethnic/tribal silver and gold

Embroidery at the State Emporia

to modern, expensive designer styles; La Boutique (www.
laboutiqueindia.com) at number 20 comes recommended,
although it tends to be pricier than some. For the experience
and the choice, go to Dariba Kalan, Old Delhi's silver bazaar,
off Chandni Chowk. As well as silver, some shops here also
sell gold and gems, though the quality and authenticity of
precious stones should be ascertained prior to purchase.

Clothes. There's not much you can't find in Delhi. Fantastic
designer items can be found in the exclusive boutiques in
South Delhi's Lodhi colony, Santushti Shopping Complex
and Hauz Khas Village (Ogaan is particularly good; www.
agaan.com). For less well-known designers, who tend to offer
interesting, experimental styles, try the shops in the village of
Shahpur Jat, on the west side of Siri Fort in South Delhi.

Venturing further south, the designer shopping complexes
near the Qutb Minar – Ambawatta Complex and Eight Mile –
are also worth a look. Head to Sarojini Nagar, in South Delhi,
where piles of cheap export rejects and past-season fashions
line the pavements, many still sporting top Western labels.
Modern Western wear is available everywhere – some of the

Tailor-made in Delhi

Delhi is a great place to buy made-to-measure clothing. There are some
very good tailoring shops in Khan Market (although some people have
reported bad experiences). Grovers had the pleasure of tailoring for
the visiting US President George W. Bush (and for Bill Clinton before
him), making it a good place to start. It's usually safer to bring a sample
to be copied, but generally they can make suits well. Another good tip
for men's suits is Tanzeb Tailors, at C36 Sujan Singh Park, just behind
Khan Market. If you're looking for Indian *salwar kameez*, then you're
better off getting them made at any of the smaller women's tailors
around the city.

Clothes shop at Hauz Khaz

best places are in South Extension Part 1 and Khan Market, again both in South Delhi.

Shops on Janpath, which runs due south from Connaught Place, and the small shops lining the streets in Paharganj's Main Bazaar, opposite New Delhi Railway Station, stock ethnic Indian clothes at rock-bottom prices, as well as some great traditional Rajasthani and Gujarati saris and scarves. Bear in mind that they deal mainly with tourists, so you'll have to haggle hard – start at least one-third lower than the asking price, and start to walk away if you're not getting the deal you want.

For simple cotton clothes, your best bet is Fabindia (www.fabindia.com) – something of an institution for Delhiites, with branches citywide (see website for details). Fabindia sells brightly coloured shirts and *kurtas* for men as well as *salwar kameez* and Western-style clothes for women. They also stock some lovely things for children at very reasonable prices. Just

A local bookshop

next door to the main Fabindia branch in Greater Kailash 1 N-Block Market, Cottons is also worth a look for its range of funky, ethnic cotton garments for men and women. Anokhi (www.anokhi.com), in Khan Market, Santushti Shopping Complex and Gurgaon, has a slightly more upmarket range of stylish, hand block-printed cotton clothes.

Cheap leather is available at Palika Bazaar, the underground market in Connaught Place, or check out Yashwant Place, a big shopping complex in Chanakyapuri which stocks every shade and style of leather jacket, fur coat and other items, all very well priced.

Shoes. If you're looking for traditional Indian jutis (camel leather slippers), try the shops on Janpath nearest Connaught Place. Bargain hard here, but don't leave empty-handed, as the quality is exceptional. For an altogether more civilised shopping experience, head for Khan Market. A favourite with the expat and diplomatic community, Khan Market has several shoe shops on the 'frontside' (facing the main road) such as Finesse, which is good for sequined shoes and heels. Other commendable options are Ashley at either Santushti Shopping Complex or Ambawatta Complex, or the many shoe shops in South Extension, including Regal or Venus Steps, which is also great for children's shoes. There are also a couple of places on Connaught Place which make shoes by hand to order, and are extremely good value.

Books. A huge number of books are printed in India every year, and there are also a massive number of imports. Khan Market is again the best place to start your browsing, with a number of good stockists, the least chaotic of which is probably Full Circle, which also has a pleasant café on the top floor. In the same district, Bahri & Sons is very popular with expats. Connaught Place also holds several well-stocked stores, the pick of which is called Bookworm (in B block). If you still haven't found what you're looking for, try The Bookshop in Jor Bagh Market, opposite Lodi Gardens, which has a fantastic range.

Antiques and furniture. One of the best selections of both antique and reproduction pieces is to be found at the centrally located Sunder Nagar Market, just south of Purana Qila. As always, Old Delhi has a lot to offer if you have the time and the patience, while almost as good value is Amar Colony in Lajpat Nagar IV, although you'll have to hunt hard to uncover the gems; there's also a lot of cheap modern stuff made here. Hauz Khas Village, in central South Delhi, has a good number of cavernous furniture stores.

Books galore

Every Sunday, an amazing book sale takes place on Darya Ganj, the road that connects the eastern end of Chandni Chowk to Delhi Gate. The pavement turns into a sea of books, with philosophy, biology, novels and comics all competing for what little space there is. There are some genuine bargains here waiting to be unearthed.

Traditional designs at the Crafts Museum

Textiles and carpets. For a wide range of textiles, try Seasons in Lajpat Nagar, or any of the huge number of shops in Nehru Place, to the southeast of town. Further out of the city, but worth the drive if you are a serious textile shopper, is Cotton and Silk at B-1, J-2/1 Mathura Road, which sells end-of-line Liberty and Conran items at very reasonable rates. For clothing fabric, Shankar Market, just to the east of Connaught Place, has a decent range.

Another good place to shop for carpets is Siva Oriental Rugs at 86A Shahpur Jat, where the emphasis is on more traditional designs. Carpet Cellar, nearby on Khel Gaon Marg, has a similar range and is a useful place to compare prices. For more contemporary designs, there are a couple of places to the south of town on the Mehrauli–Gurgaon Road, of which Hands has been recommended.

Handicrafts. Shops selling handicrafts of various types can be found throughout Delhi. For one of the city's more relaxed shopping experiences, head for Dilli Haat, opposite INA Market in South Delhi. It's a government-run initiative where you pay a small fee to enter and then have 100 or so crafts stalls to choose from, as well as a good selection of eateries offering a variety of cuisines from all over India. Different events and collections take place every month or two, but Dilli Haat is worth a visit at any time of the year. Another good place to go for a wide range of handicrafts is Surajkund Mela, an annual fair that takes place in February (see page 98). Hauz Khas Village in central South Delhi is a great place to pick up artworks, especially Bollywood film posters.

NIGHTLIFE AND ENTERTAINMENT

Although things have definitely improved over the last decade or so, Delhi is still not the world's most happening capital city. Draconian drinking laws are partly to blame. Also a factor is

Delhi's emporia

Particularly useful if you only have a short time in Delhi and a numbers of things to buy, the Cottage Industries Emporium (www.cottage emporiumindia.com) on Janpath, just south of Connaught Place, is something of an institution. It's essentially a department store of goods from all over India, and while the prices may not be as keen as elsewhere, there's an unbeatable range on offer and minimal hassle involved – everything carries a price tag and haggling is unheard of. There's also a long row of State Emporia on Baba Kharak Singh Marag, again close to Connaught Place, which offer specialities from every state in India. While there are some interesting products on sale, the presentation tends to be a little uninspiring, and the government-employed staff are not overly concerned with standards of service.

the fickle nature of the local 'in' crowd, which tends to frequent a place only for the first few weeks it's open, moving on as soon as another establishment opens its doors. This means that many bars and clubs have a very short shelf life, often closing after less than a year. The upshot is that some of the places listed here, while generally reasonably well established, may have ceased to be by the time this book is released, so check locally before setting out.

Nightclubs

Delhi's only nightclub that would not look out of place in the West is Elevate (www.elevateindia.com), spread over four levels of Centre Stage Mall in NOIDA (see page 67), on the east bank of the Yamuna River. With a sound system and video installations imported from London, it's the biggest, trendiest club in India. International DJs often

Live music at Connaught Place

do guest spots at the weekends, although the house DJ knows his stuff as well. Expect a mix of fairly commercial house, hip hop and trance, with Bollywood mixes on Fridays; cool off on the rooftop terrace when it gets too hot on the 600-person dancefloor.

Cocktails at Q'Ba

Agni at The Park, 15 Parliament Street, is Connaught Place's most consistently happening nightspot, boasting interiors by Conran and staff in sexy Rohit Bal designer outfits. It's popular with the city's A-listers and serves up a mix of hip hop and Bollywood, though drink prices are exorbitant.

In the same league are Decibel in the Hotel Samrat on Kautilya Marg, Chanakyapuri, which pulls in hip young expats from the nearby diplomatic enclave on weekends. Also, SoHo, a cavernous Asian-themed lounge at the Ashok Hotel in Chanakyapuri, where DJs play hip hop, R&B and Bollywood mixes. Despite the bare pipes still jutting from the walls, the overall effect is easy on the eye and pleasingly luxurious. It's a great place early in the evening, before the music gets cranked up too high and conversation ceases to be a viable option. The rest of the 'nightclub' establishments are basically bars with a small dance floor attached.

Bars
There are a wide variety of watering holes in Delhi. Connaught Place has a fair number of appealing options, ranging from the swanky Q'Ba (42 E Block), with its Q-shaped bar, comfy leather furniture and rooftop terrace,

Bars on a budget

Pahar Ganj is where you'll find some of Delhi's cheapest bars. A few of them actually have licences; others may serve you in a more circumspect manner – don't be surprised if your beer turns up in a cup and saucer!

to the more pub-style DV8 in the Regal Building. Also on Connaught Place are the cheap and cheerful Regent's Blues (18 N Block) and Rodeo (12 A Block). United Coffee House (15 E Block; despite the name it's more than just a café) has lengthy happy hours and good-value pitchers of beer.

Those wanting a more refined drinking experience should head for the 1911 bar in the Imperial Hotel on Janpath. With a solid colonial feel and comfortable leather upholstery, this is one of the city's most upmarket drinking establishments, offering an unbeatable range of drinks from far and wide. The city's more fashionable bars are in South Delhi, generally in the main shopping markets. Greater Kailash 1's N-Block Market has the best variety; Bohemia, in a restaurant and café complex called Kasbah, is one of the few genuine bars in town – most are restaurants as well. It has a pleasantly relaxed feel, friendly staff and an understanding DJ, a rare combination which makes this place stand out. Almost next door you will find Urban Pind, which has a similar 'lounge' atmosphere to Bohemia, only on a larger scale, with three separate floors and in-your-face erotic Khajuraho bas reliefs decorating the walls. They also serve excellent Indian and Italian cuisine. Longer established, but still one of the most popular hangouts in town, is Shalom (www.shalomexperience.com), more or less opposite Kasbah. Served against a backdrop of wooden furniture and whitewashed walls, the food is Mediterranean, with an emphasis on Lebanese dishes, the music mellow and there is always a lively crowd.

Calypso, part of the Bistro building in Hauz Khas Village, is another stylish spot for a drink either before or after dinner in the rooftop restaurant. There's another good clutch of bars across South Delhi in the Basant Lok complex in Vasant Vihar, including the Hookah Bar, which offers lots of shishas to puff on; and the über-suave Kylinn, with malt whiskies, Cuban cigars and a terrific sushi menu to boot.

Evening comes to Gurgaon

Cultural life

Delhi boasts a rich and varied cultural life to complement its nightlife offerings, with one or other of the city's galleries and auditoriums always having something of interest to see. The India Habitat Centre (www.indiahabitat.org; see page 56) hosts a wide range of dance, music, film and theatre, as well as art exhibitions. The Kamani Auditorium (www.kamaniauditorium.org) on Copernicus Marg, near Mandi House metro station, stages performances of classical Indian dance and music, as well as art exhibitions. If you fancy catching the latest Bollywood offering, or a Hollywood blockbuster, head for any of the PVR cinemas – the Plaza on Connaught Place, a renovated old cinema hall, is particularly good. For detailed listings grab a copy of *First City* magazine, available at newsstands across the capital.

SPORTS

Much like the rest of India, Delhi is cricket mad. International matches are played at the Kotla Stadium, but less formal matches take place every minute of the day, every day of the year. Watching any other type of sport is anathema to most Indians; the next best thing in Delhi is probably polo, with matches throughout the winter season at the Delhi Racing Club behind Safdarjung's Tomb.

There are several public swimming pools in Delhi; the most convenient is probably the NMDC Pool at Nehru Park in Chanakyapuri. Most of the city's plusher hotels have pools, and some of them allow non-guests to swim in them, but often for an exorbitant fee. There's also a well-maintained 18-hole golf course open to non-members, Delhi Golf Club (tel: 011-2436 2768) on Dr Zakir Hussain Marg.

Party balloons in Lodi Gardens

CHILDREN'S DELHI

The range of activities to keep the kids amused in Delhi will largely depend on the time of year. Of the outdoor attractions that may be ruled out by the heat during summer, Delhi Zoo (Sat–Thur 9.30am–4pm; charge) is one of the best. While it's not up to international standards, the animals look reasonably happy and there's plenty of room for kids to run around. Star draws are the monkeys, hippos, giraffes and cheetahs, although the biggest squeals are reserved for the impressive-looking white tigers. The zoo is close to Purana Qila, southeast of India Gate. There's a boating lake next door which might also appeal to younger visitors.

There are a couple of museums that are particularly good for kids. One of them is the Science Museum, part of the Pragati Maidan complex east of India Gate, which has a fair number of push-button, interactive displays, as well as a walk-through dinosaur jungle. Shankar's International Dolls Museum (Tue–Sun 10am–6pm; charge), part of the Nehru House complex at 4 Bahadur Shah Zafar Marg, is an absolute doll fest, with 6,500 of the smiling cuties from all over the world.

These, and others, feature on a great programme of tours, workshops and courses run by a team called FlowIndia (http://flowindia.wordpress.com/) which aims to get youngsters interested in the wealth of art and museum attractions in and around the capital.

Delhi has a good number of parks, most of which have some sort of children's playground, but easily the pick of the bunch is the Children's Park at India Gate, with more swings and slides than the rest of the parks put together. The Garden of Five Senses (see page 65) is another place that should keep children entertained for a while, as is the National Rail Museum (see page 50).

Another possibility is the Children's Riding Club (www.childrensridingclub.com) just behind Safdarjung's Tomb, where kids can have a ride around a paddock on some suitably small ponies, and run round the small farm next door. About the best option when the weather is too hot to be outdoors is Little Buddie's Planet in Ansal Plaza shopping centre on Khel Gaon Marg. It's an indoor play area boasting slides and ball pools, but best of all, it's air-conditioned.

Calendar of Events

There are hundreds of festivals in Delhi every year, often taking place in only one part of the city, or among one particular community. Those listed below are the main events.

January *Lohri Festival* celebrates the peak of winter, and is marked by bonfires, singing and dancing. 26 January is Republic Day, celebrated with a parade of military might, folk dancing and colourful floats.

February *Surajkund Crafts Mela* is a huge crafts fair held at Surajkund, 5km (3 miles) south of Tughlaqabad. Delhi Tourism organises a Garden Festival at the Garden of Five Senses. *Jahan-i-Khusrau*, a Sufi music festival, takes place in the grounds of Humayun's Tomb.

March *Holi* marks the end of winter and the onset of spring, and is celebrated by throwing coloured paint or *gulal* powder mixed with water at friends, neighbours and passers-by.

15 August is *Independence Day*, marked by particularly animated celebrations at Red Fort, where a flag is ritually raised to signify India's independence from British rule.

October *Phulwalon-Ki-Sair*, or the Flower Sellers' Procession, centres around the Qutb Minar, aimed at promoting communal harmony; it is celebrated by both Hindus and Muslims. *Dussehra* marks Rama's triumph over the demon Ravana, of whom huge effigies are made and then ritually burnt on the last of the 10 days of the festival; often packed with fireworks, the effigies literally go up with a bang. The *Qutb Festival* of classical music and dance takes place at the Qutb Minar complex, with performances from some of the country's best artists.

November *Diwali* (Deepavali), the festival of lights and fireworks, celebrates Rama and Sita's homecoming after their exile in the *Ramayana*. Festivities include illuminating houses by the lighting of oil lamps and firecrackers, and the exchanging of sweets and gifts.

Moveable feast: Ramadan, the Muslim month of fasting, moves back by about 11 days each year. *Id-ul-Fitr* marks the end of Ramadan, and is particularly heartily celebrated in Old Delhi.

EATING OUT

While the quality of Delhi's Indian cuisine restaurants and food stalls has never been in doubt, recent years have seen a significant hike in the quality and variety of international offerings, making Delhi a real gourmet destination at last. Punjabi influence has permeated much of Delhi's daily life, and the food is no exception. Although typically heavy on the butter and *ghee* (clarified butter), good Punjabi dishes are uniquely filling, yet full of surprisingly delicate and varied tastes. The same dish is never the same twice, and in some cases can be entirely different from one restaurant, or *dhaba*, to another.

Delhi's famous street food

Vegetarian dishes tend to revolve around *dal* (lentils) in either black or yellow guise, *paneer* (often translated as cottage cheese, it has a similarly neutral taste but is more tofu-like in texture) and green vegetables including spinach, peas, okra, capsicum and cauliflower. Chicken, and 'butter chicken' in particular, is the standard 'non-veg' offering, with mutton often an option as well.

Mughlai cuisine is quite similar to Punjabi but ostensibly more sophisticated,

A fine Mughlai spread

the recipes having been handed down from the kitchens of the Moghul emperors. While the very best exponents of the Mughlai school produce a variety and combination of different tastes and textures that are nothing short of exquisite, there are a number of Punjabi restaurants aimed at tourists which have simply rebranded their standard fare as Mughlai in a bid to justify inflated prices.

South Indian cuisine is not especially well represented in Delhi, although there are a number of simple eateries that do a reasonable job of the ubiquitous *masala dosa*, an outsized savoury pancake made from fermented rice-flour batter that's rolled into a tube and filled with a combination of potato, onions, coconut, chilli and mustard seeds – an absolute treat when you come across a good one. There are also a couple of South Indian chains with a limited but competent range on offer. Mumbai's street snacks get a much better deal, with the most popular staples such as *pao bhaji* (a red-lentil-and-tomato-based sauce accompanied by a white bread roll) and *bhel puri* (puffed rice, vermicelli, potato and *puri*-style bread mixed with onions, tomatoes, coriander and lemon juice) available from stalls all over the city.

Seafood is similarly hard to get hold of; traditional wisdom dictates that in a place this far from the sea, the freshness of fish in the summer months must be open to question. Having said that, there are a number of specialist restaurants which fly their produce in daily, and are well worth trying.

The number-one non-Indian cuisine is without doubt Chinese. A word of warning: Indian restaurants tend to be very ambitious in the range and scope of the dishes that they offer. Indeed, few mid-range places offer just one type of cuisine; a menu with a vast array of Indian, Chinese and Continental dishes is pretty much the norm. The reality, however, is that all the dishes served in this type of 'multi-cuisine' restaurant will generally have something of India in them, with both the Chinese and Continental offerings likely to be liberally laced with Indian spices. Dishes such as pasta or even salads are often dismissed as 'bland' unless enlivened with liberal lashings of chilli powder – you have been warned!

There are, however, a number of exceptional Chinese eateries, generally distinguishable by the lack of Indian dishes on their menus, as well as some excellent Italian, Greek, Lebanese and 'fusion' restaurants. Happily for the wallets of the upmarket Delhi diner, these places are no longer found solely in the city's five-star hotels, a development which has much improved the dining scene.

After the astronomical price of some of the accommodation, the generally reasonable price of eating out should come as a welcome surprise. Some of the dhabas offer amazing value for money, serving filling meals for less than Rs100, and

The Big Chill café in Khan market

some world-class restaurants cost a fraction of their equivalents in the West. While most of the dhabas stay open all day, the pricier places will open for lunch at noon, close again at 3pm and then reopen at 7pm for dinner, closing at around 11pm–midnight.

WHERE TO EAT

Breakfast

Travellers from the West are often surprised to learn that what they would call 'curry' is eaten by Indians even at breakfast. Favourites include *puri* and *paratha*, a fried, flat bread most commonly stuffed with potato and green chillies and served with some sort of 'chutney'. These are not chutneys as Westerners know them, but instead fiery concoctions aimed at adding zest to a meal, to be consumed in small quantities.

Muesli is a definite long shot, although cornflakes are start-ing to be more widespread, and will certainly be on the menu of most backpacker establishments. 'Jam, butter, toast' is some-thing of a classic in the more touristy areas – bear in mind that the bread will always be white, and generally 'toasted' in a pan rather than a toaster or grill. Eggs are also not hard to find, although only a *masala* (chilli-charged) omelette is likely to meet with local approval.

Those whose idea of breakfast is more along the coffee-and-pastry line will not be disappointed, with new coffee bars springing up all over (see below).

Lunch

There's a massive array of options for eating in the middle of the day, although some travellers may find the Punjabi-style dishes slightly heavy for a midday meal. *Thalis*, a large metal dish with a combination of rice and bread in its centre, sur-rounded by up to 10 small metal bowls containing a wide variety of both sweet and savoury dishes, can make an excel-lent alternative. Not only very good value, they're also a great way of tasting a lot of dishes at the same time, and working out which ones you particularly like. They're to be found at both North and South Indian restaurants, and often change on a daily basis.

Delhi boasts an increasingly large number of Starbucks and Costa-style coffee shop chains. Domestic contenders include the well-established Barista brand, along with Café Coffee Day, Barista's younger, slightly cheaper but less classy competitor. Both serve a range of Western-style snacks which make a perfectly acceptable lunchtime meal, particularly in the heat of the summer, but are in no way comparable to a good deli sandwich.

Those pining for an authentic fast-food experience need not worry; McDonald's, Pizza Hut and Subway, to name but

Chor Bizarre restaurant

a few, have outlets in many locations in the city. There are also a few independent, Western-style café/restaurants which are beginning to hit their stride. These are mainly to be found in the more upmarket shopping areas – Khan Market probably has the best range.

Dinner

Dinnertime is when Delhi really gets going as a place to eat out. There's a tastebud-tingling selection of experiences on offer, both in terms of food and settings. You can eat from a buffet arranged in a converted car in Old Delhi, enjoy good quality Thai from a rooftop overlooking the Qutb Minar, eat mouth-watering Mughlai cuisine overlooking floodlit Moghul monuments, or enjoy the finest of fine dining aboard a faithful replica of the Orient Express.

Most restaurants lack such views or surroundings, but the quality of the food more than makes up for this. The standard of North Indian cuisine is generally high, with good options in most areas, while more careful selection will lead you to a dependable range of non-Indian eateries. Delhiites on the whole eat much later than their counterparts in Northern Europe or North America. Restaurants generally open for dinner at 7pm, but very few customers arrive before 9pm. For listings of restaurants, see Places to Eat, page 108.

Drinks

Mineral water is served everywhere, although technically this is a misnomer. All but two of the brands available are actually filtered tap water; only the Himalayan and the rare and very expensive Evian brands are bottled at a mountain source. They are all, however, safe to drink as long as the plastic seal around the lid is unbroken. The same is true of all bottled soft drinks, although some of the local brands can be sickly sweet.

Chai (sweet milk tea) is served everywhere, and is again safe to imbibe. It generally comes in 'ready-made' form available everywhere but in the smartest restaurants. This means that cut tea leaves are boiled together with milk and sugar to produce an invigorating and much-loved beverage. Those in search of a 'real' coffee should head to one of the many Starbucks-style cafés that have sprung up all over the city.

Lassi, a yoghurt-based drink often served after a meal, or as a refreshing snack at other times, can take some getting used to, but is invaluable for its cooling properties, particularly after a spicy meal. It comes in all sorts of flavours; plain, sweet or salty are the basic options, but specialist *lassiwallahs* will have a whole range on offer.

Alcohol is fairly easy to come by, increasingly in restaurants as well as bars. Both local and imported beers and spirits are widely available, with wine starting to gain popularity. Indian producers are now making wine which is, if not world-class, certainly very drinkable and significantly cheaper than imported wine, which tends to be available only in the five-star hotels. Labels to look out for include Sula, Grover, Indage, York and, if you're in the mood for something bubbly, Marquise de Pompadour. Both beer and wine bottles will be presented to you prior to being opened. This is not so you can ascertain the vintage of your brew, but rather to confirm to the waiter by touching the bottle that the contents are sufficiently chilled.

TO HELP YOU READ THE MENU...

Meat/Fish

gosht	meat, often mutton	**macchli**	fish
jhinga	prawns	**murg**	chicken

Vegetables

aloo	potato	**mutter**	peas
bhindi	okra	**piaza**	onion
brinjal/baigan	aubergine	**pudina**	mint
chana	chickpeas	**saag/palak**	spinach
dal	lentils	**rajma**	red kidney beans
gobhi	cauliflower		
khumb	mushroom	**zeera**	cumin

Dairy products

dahi	curd/yoghurt	**malai**	cream
ghee	clarified butter	**paneer**	cheese
makhan	butter	**raita**	savoury yoghurt

Breads

naan	thicker, doughier white-flour flatbread
parantha	layered flatbread fried in *ghee*
roti/chapati	unleavened wholewheat-flour flatbread

Preparations

biryani	rice mixed with meat or vegetables and flavoured with saffron
kadhai	dish cooked in a deep, round pan, or *kadhai*
kofta	dumpling or ball
masala	marinated in spices
pulao/pilau	rice fried with spices, fruit, nuts or vegetables
shahi	dish made with dried fruit or nuts
tandoori	dry preparation cooked in a clay oven

Food from every state at Dilli Haat

Snacks

masala dosa	South Indian pancake rolled into a tube and stuffed with potato, onions, coconut, chilli and mustard seeds
papad/ poppadom	thin, crispy bread made from ground lentils, often flavoured with cumin
pakora	small piece of vegetable or *paneer* deep-fried in chickpea-flour batter
samosa	deep-fried parcel of spiced meat or vegetables

Sweets

gulab jamun	deep-fried dough balls soaked in syrup
jalebi	spirals of deep-fried, syrup-soaked batter
kheer	India's rice pudding equivalent
kulfi	pistachio-flavoured ice cream-like dessert
halwa	sweetmeat of vegetables, fruit, nuts and sugar

PLACES TO EAT

The price ranges quoted below are per person, and include one alcoholic beverage with your meal in the Rs500 and over ranges:

$$$$$** over Rs1,000   **$$$$ Rs500–1,000
$$$** Rs300–500   **$$ Rs100–300
$ under Rs100

OLD DELHI

Chor Bizarre $$$$ *Hotel Broadway, 4/15A Asaf Ali Road, tel: 2327 3821, www.chorbizarrerestaurant.com.* Reliably delicious Mughlai and Kashmiri fare in quirky surroundings. The salad buffet is housed in a classic car, while the tables are made from all manner of curios, including a four-poster bed. Reservations highly recommended.

Karim's $$ *Gali Kebabiyan (just south of Jama Masjid), tel: 2326 4981, www.karimhoteldelhi.com.* 'Secret of good mood, taste of Karim's food' says the menu of this Old Delhi institution, hidden away in the intense Jama Masjid area of the city, and judging by the number of satisfied customers, they can't be far wrong. Most people come for the legendary roti kebabs, but they do a huge menu of traditional, meaty tandoori dishes and slow-baked biryanis. Not recommended for vegetarians.

Moti Mahal $$$ *3704 Netaji Subhash Marg, Daryaganj, tel: 2327 3661.* If you would rather enjoy your Mughlai cuisine in more refined surroundings, this is the place to go. For many years the standard bearer in the world of Delhi's North Indian restaurants (it allegedly invented tandoori-butter-chicken-masala), MM still serves food of a consistently high quality, in its soothingly calm, if somewhat dimly lit, interior.

PAHAR GANJ

Appetite $ *1575 Main Bazaar.* Tempting Nepali, Indian and Italian fare. The *lassis* are really special, and the pastries not bad either.

Malhotra Restaurant $ *Top end of Main Bazaar.* Astounding range of cuisines but all done to a reasonably high standard, including tandoor, Mughlai and South Indian, as well as Continental and Chinese.

Metropolis $$ *Metropolis Hotel, 1634 Main Bazaar, tel: 5154 1395.* This popular rooftop restaurant is one of the most reliable places to eat in Pahar Ganj, serving up a good spread of north Indian fare, plus assorted European offerings and cheap cold beer.

Sam's Café $ *Vivek Hotel, 1534–50 Main Bazaar, tel: 4154 1437.* The strident interior marks this place out as modern, but for a quick bite it's as good as anywhere, with a range of Indian and European fare aimed at passing backpacker trade.

CONNAUGHT PLACE AND AROUND

Kake Da Hotel $ *74 Municipal Market, Outer Ring, Connaught Place, tel: 2341 1580.* A simple but well-established and perennially popular Punjabi *dhaba*. The food here is dependably tasty and extremely good value, which, combined with the lightning-quick service, makes this place a winner. Try their famous chicken curry, mopped up with piping hot rotis.

Q'BA $$$$ *F-42/43, Connaught Place, tel: 4517 3333, www.qba. co.in.* One of the trendier joints in town, this is a cavernous but comfortable space serving a variety of tasty Indian, Italian and Thai fare in super-stylish surroundings, arranged over three floors.

Rodeo $$$ *A12 Connaught Place, tel: 2371 3780.* Unpretentious, good-value Tex-Mex bar-restaurant featuring Wild West decor and cheap beer, plus cowboy waiters and tequila shots – quite a spectacle.

Saravana Bhawan $$ *46 Janpath, tel: 2331 6060, and P15 Connaught Circus, tel: 2334 7755.* Delhi branches of the popular nationwide chain, serving good examples of all the South Indian staples, including the city's biggest and best *masala dosas* and interesting *thalis*.

Spice Route $$$$$ *Imperial Hotel, Janpath, tel: 2334 1234.* While there may be restaurants serving better oriental food, no other place can match the grandeur of Spice Route. Seven years in the making, this exceptional work of art comprises minutely carved wooden panels and arches taken from dismantled Thai temples. While the Southeast Asian and Keralan food can't quite match the splendour of the surroundings, this restaurant still makes for a special treat.

Spirit $$$$ *E34, Inner Circle, Connaught Place (1st floor), tel: 4101 7006.* Classy bar/restaurant offering some of the best Mediterranean food around – Lebanese is a speciality. They also have a better wine list than most.

United Coffee House $$$ *E15 Connaught Place, tel: 2341 1697.* The food is only part of the attraction here – it's the original cake-icing decor and the faded 1940s ambience that everyone comes for. The menu is long and eclectic, and the beer cold and well priced.

Véda $$$$$ *H27 Outer Circle, Connaught Place, tel: 4151 3535.* Decorated by one of Delhi's leading fashion designers, Véda is where the A-list come to schmooze over fussy neo-Indian cuisine. Its candlelit, baroque-style interior sets a lavish tone. The food frequently fails to live up to the sky-high prices, but the glossy party vibe is why Delhi's glitterati flock here.

Yamu's Panchayat $$ *92 NDMC Market, Connaught Place.* The only 100 percent hygienic place in the capital where you can sample the full range of authentic paan, prepared and, a first for the city, served by women. Come in a group and you can order the house speciality – *paan aadab* – seven individual paans wrapped in one big leaf. Everything's beautifully presented and fresh, and honey is used rather than sugar as a sweetener.

SOUTH DELHI

Basil & Thyme $$ *Santushti Shopping Complex, tel: 2467 3322.* Lively bistro-style café-restaurant, popular with Delhi's ladies-who-lunch and visiting diplomats for its eclectic menu of artfully prepared Mediterranean dishes with world-cuisine fusion influences. Hostess, celeb-chef Bhicoo Manekshaw, runs a tight ship, despite being well into her eighties. Closes at 6pm.

Big Chill $$ *35 and 68A Khan Market, tel: 4175 7588.* Superlative range of Italian dishes plus desserts and home-made ice cream to die for, served against Hollywood-inspired decor. The menu is vast, featuring Indian, Chinese and continental dishes, and the atmosphere lively, particularly at weekends, when you may have to queue for a table.

Bohème $$$ *6th Floor, 22 Hauz Khas Village, South Delhi.* This studiously boho, Italian-style rooftop café in the arty Hauz Khas Village enclave serves tempting meze and sunny Mediterranean salads under thatched gazebos and wood-floored lounge areas, but the tranquil views over the lake and treetops are its main selling point. Ask your way to the more famous Gunpowder Restaurant – Bohème is on the floor above.

Bukhara $$$$$ *Sheraton Maurya Hotel, Sardar Patel Marg, tel: 2611 2233.* Bukhara is the long-established king of the North-West Frontier, or at least its cuisine. Catering chiefly to the carnivore, the dishes here are melt-in-the-mouth tender, and spiced to perfection. Advance bookings essential, especially at weekends.

Café Turtle $$ *Full Circle Bookshop, 5B Khan Market, tel: 2465 5641, www.cafeturtle.com.* Cosy little bookshop café-diner, decorated in sunny Mediterranean colours, with a menu to match: they're big on pasta, Moroccan light bites, pittas, felafels and filled sandwiches – and the cakes are legendary.

Flavors $$$$ *C52 Moolchand Flyover Complex, Defence Colony, tel: 2464 5644* Italian-owned and run, Flavors dishes up some of the most authentic Italian cuisine in town with huge portions of great pasta, risotto and wood-fired pizza, plus irresistible desserts. The garden terrace is still the place to sit, making this a better place for lunch than dinner.

Havemore $$ *11–12 Pandara Road Market, tel: 2338 7070.* One of the best of the handful of upmarket *dhabas* in Pandara Market, with a good selection of North Indian dishes and a convenient location just south of India Gate – useful if you've been sightseeing around Rajpath.

Lodi The Garden Restaurant $$$$ *Lodi Gardens, Lodi Road, tel: 2465 5054.* This restaurant enjoys a wonderful location in the serene Lodi Gardens. Its expansive terrace is the biggest draw, although the Mediterranean and Lebanese food comes a close second. Sunday brunch makes for a particularly pleasant experience.

Oh! Calcutta $$$ *E Block, International Trade Towers, Nehru Place, tel: 2646 4180.* Delhi's first real attempt at bringing the cuisine of West Bengal to the capital's diners. The emphasis is squarely on sea- and river food – try the *kangra chingri bhapa*, Thai-style steam cakes wrapped in banana leaves, filled with crab and prawns and flavoured with lime and mustard.

Olive Bar & Kitchen $$$$$ *Haveli No. 6–8, One Style Mile, Kalka Dass Marg, Mehrauli, tel: 2664 5500.* One of the city's best Mediterranean eateries; the menu is varied and consistently of a high standard, the service is discreet but polished and the decor superb. Set in a whitewashed old *haveli*, with a choice of dining inside or out, this could almost be a villa on the Med. Has been a hit with Delhi's smart set since day one – don't even think of going without a reservation.

Orient Express $$$$$ *Taj Palace Hotel, 2 Sardar Patel Marg, tel: 2611 0202.* The finest of traditional fine dining that the city has to offer, and certainly the only place where your seven-course meal will be served in a stationary railway carriage. The menu features dishes from all the countries which the Orient Express train would have passed through, with the emphasis on classic French haute cuisine, and they offer an award-winning wine list

Parikrama $$$ *22 Kasturba Gandhi Marg, tel: 2372 1616.* Delhi's first revolving restaurant (it takes 90 minutes to complete a full revolution), offering a mix of Indian and Chinese food, plus memorable bird's-eye views over Delhi, best appreciated during the day.

Ploof $$$$ *13 Main Market, Lodi Colony, tel: 2464 9026.* One of the city's few seafood specialists, and easily the best. Fish is flown in daily, so you need not fret about freshness, and some of the preparations are sublime, particularly those from South India. Try the benchmark Singapore chilli crab.

Punjabi by Nature $$$ *11 Basant Lok Complex, Vasant Vihar, tel: 4151 6666.* The ultimate in Punjabi cuisine, the food at this place gets consistently rave reviews, and is hugely popular with locals – worth booking ahead, especially at weekends.

Sagar $ *18 Defence Colony Market, tel: 2433 3440.* Delhi's most acclaimed South Indian eatery is famous above all for serving the city's largest, crispest dosas: order a 'family dosa', and you'll be brought a 4-foot-long monster which has to be carried by two waiters. The rest of the menu relies more on fabulous southern flavours than visual impact to impress; everything's tasty, the service supreme, and prices more than fair.

Swagath $$$ *14 Defence Colony Market, tel: 2433 7538.* Under the same management as nearby Sagar, this South Indian seafood restaurant maintains the same high standards as its close neighbour. The slightly functional interior and bright lights are soon forgotten once the food arrives, although don't make the mistake of ordering anything but fish.

Terrace in the Sky $$$$ *The Village Bistro Complex, 12 Hauz Khas Village, tel: 2685 3857.* There are a number of restaurants in this complex, but the pick of them is on the roof terrace, overlooking the floodlit remains of medieval Siri. The food is upmarket Mughlai, and very tasty it is too, but the exotic views are what you'll savour longest.

Thai Wok $$$$ *Top Floor, Ambawatta Shopping Complex, Mehrauli, tel: 2664 4289.* The beautifully decorated roof terrace overlooking the Qutb Minar, the soft lighting and ambient music all help you to unwind before you even look at the menu. The Thai cuisine doesn't disappoint either, being authentically fiery, and the portions are huge. Definitely worth the journey to get there.

Threesixty $$$$$ *Oberoi Hotel, Dr Zakir Hussain Marg, tel: 2436 3030.* The city's hippest restaurant, and in a lot of ways its most refined – with prices to match. The interior is cutting-edge contemporary, as are the glass-fronted kitchens, where an amazing variety of Japanese, Continental and Indian delicacies are rustled up before your eyes.

A–Z TRAVEL TIPS

A Summary of Practical Information

A

ACCOMMODATION

Delhi suffers from an acute shortage of quality accommodation. The biggest lack is in the middle price range. There are the usual five-star offerings, which are so in demand from November to February that they are able to charge outlandish rates, and a huge glut of rock-bottom budget places, mostly centred around the traditional backpacker haven of Pahar Ganj. Karol Bagh, slightly further to the west but still within striking distance of Connaught Place, is gaining popularity with the upper end of the budget market. From there to the four stars is a big jump, but it is filled by a few pleasant hotels in Sunder Nagar, not far from India Gate, and some relaxing converted home-type guesthouses and stylish upper-mid-range B&Bs. The whole city can become fully booked during the winter months, when the tourist season is at its peak, making life difficult for anyone arriving without a reservation.

AIRPORT

Despite massive infrastructural improvements ahead of the 2010 Commonwealth Games, Delhi's airports continue to fall foul with frustrating regularity to the extremities of north India's weather. The situation becomes particularly severe in January, when fog sometimes prevents planes from taking off until 11am, by which time there's a huge backlog.

Indira Gandhi International Airport (DEL; tel: 011 2567 5126; www.delhiairport.com) is 19km (12 miles) southwest of the city centre; the domestic terminal (tel: 011 2565 2011) is a further 5km (3 miles) away at Palam. On arriving at the international airport, the best transport options into the city are either the very reasonable but slow bus, or prepaid taxi. There are numerous kiosks to the left as you come out of security, but ignore them all; the official, and cheapest, taxi service has its office just outside the door to the right as you exit. It's also worth remembering that luggage is not left to travel round and round the carousel, but taken off and arranged on the floor next to the relevant belt.

The domestic terminal at Palam is crying out for expansion, with as many as half the flights in and out routinely delayed. Be sure to check your flight's status before leaving for the airport, especially if you're travelling on one of the newer budget airlines, which are fantastic value but always seem to get the short straw when it comes to flight slots.

B

BEGGING

As a foreign traveller in Delhi you'll become a frequent target for the city's numerous beggars, who congregate at traffic lights and tourist hot spots, such as Connaught Place. Whether to give is a personal decision; if you do feel like giving, a few rupees is sufficient.

BUDGETING FOR YOUR TRIP

Delhi is by no means dirt-cheap. Here are a few examples of costs to give you an idea how much money you're likely to need:

Airport transfer. Prepaid taxi from international airport to centre of town: Rs350 (£4.50/\$7).

Accommodation. A double room in mid-range hotel, including all taxes: Rs3,500 (£45/\$70) per night.

Meals. A cooked breakfast at your hotel costs Rs300 (£4/\$6), dinner at an expensive restaurant, including a bottle of beer, Rs2,000 (£25/\$40).

Sightseeing. Entrance charges vary enormously. At smaller attractions, you'll probably pay around Rs50 (£0.60/\$1), or less, while at more high-profile sites entrance charges usually run between (£1.50/\$2) and Rs250 (£3.50/\$5). The major exception is the Taj Mahal, for which you'll have to fork out Rs750 (£9.50/\$15), unless you're Indian, in which case it costs just Rs20 (£0.30/\$0.40).

C

CAR HIRE

While it is becoming increasingly possible to hire self-drive cars in Delhi, it is actually significantly cheaper to hire one with a driver and, unless you really can't do without the 'Delhi driving' experience, a whole lot less stressful. Traffic conventions are not so much flouted as ignored, signposts are a rarity and road names seldom marked, making driving yourself around quite an ordeal. All hotels will be able to arrange a car with a driver. A car with driver costs Rs1,000 (£12.50/$20) per day without air conditioning, Rs3,000 (£26/$60) with air conditioning, plus an additional cost for any distance over 100km (60 miles).

CLIMATE

Delhi has one of the world's more wildly fluctuating climates. While summers can be unbearably hot, with temperatures sometimes climbing into the mid-40s°C (110s°F), winters can be surprisingly cold. The city's proximity to the Himalayas ensures that night-time winter temperatures can get down to freezing point and the city can suffer from freezing fogs. One positive point is that humidity remains low for most of the year, with only the build-up to the monsoon and the rainy season (July–Aug) itself feeling especially humid. The most pleasant months are Nov–Feb, when nights are cool enough to sleep without air conditioning or a fan, but days are still bright and sunny.

CLOTHING

What you wear will be largely dictated by the timing of your visit. The pronounced difference in day- and night-time temperatures from September to March means that you'll need both light and warm clothes, while from April to August you'll rarely need long sleeves, even at night. Indians tend to dress more formally than their counterparts in the West. Attitudes are beginning to change, however, especially among the affluent classes, where jeans, T shirts and suntops are the norm, although women should be careful to cover up, particularly in Old Delhi and other Muslim areas.

CRIME AND SAFETY

Although Delhi generally feels a safe place to be, women on their own should take extra care. The pernicious male adolescent pastime of 'Eve-teasing' (public sexual harassment), which takes the form of lewd comments to stroking or even grabbing of female body parts, while rarely done with any serious intent, is obviously a cause for concern. Muggings are rare, although there have been isolated cases of rape.

Take the same precautions as you would at home. If you are unlucky enough to have something stolen, bear in mind that you'll have to report the theft to the police within 24 hours in order to be able to make an insurance claim (see page 127).

E

ELECTRICITY

Power supply is 220V 50Hz AC, via two- or three-pin round plugs. European visitors should be able to run their appliances using a simple adaptor, widely available locally, while those from the US may also need a transformer.

EMBASSIES AND HIGH COMMISSIONS

In Delhi
Australian High Commission Australian Compound, 1-50G Shantipath, Chanakyapuri, New Delhi (PO Box 5210); tel: 011-4139 9900; www.india.embassy.gov.au.
British High Commission Shantipath, Chanakyapuri, New Delhi; tel: 011-2687 2161; http://ukinindia.fco.gov.uk.
Canadian High Commission 7–8 Shantipath, Chanakyapuri, New

Delhi (PO Box 5207); tel: 011-4178 2000; ww.canadainternational.gc.ca.

Irish Embassy 230 Jor Bagh; tel: 011-2462 6733; www.irelandinindia.com.

New Zealand High Commission 50N Nyaya Marg, Chanakyapuri, New Delhi; tel: 011-2688 3170; www.nzembassy.com/india.

US Embassy Shantipath, Chanakyapuri, New Delhi; tel: 011-2419 8000; http://newdelhi.usembassy.gov.

Indian Missions Abroad

Australia High Commission: 3–5 Moonah Place, Yarralumla, Canberra, ACT 2600; tel: 02-6273 3999; www.hcindia-au.org.

Canada High Commission: 10 Springfield Rd, Ottawa, ON, K1M 1C9; tel: 613-744 3751; www.hciottawa.ca.

UK High Commission: India House, Aldwych, London WC2B 4NA, tel: 020-7632 3149, http://hcilondon.in.

US Embassy of India (Consular Services): 2536 Massachusetts Ave NW, Washington DC 20008, tel: 202-939 7000, www.indianembassy.org.

EMERGENCIES

Police 100
Fire 101
Ambulance 102

For medical requirements, the best hospital in town is the Apollo, on Mathura Road near Tughlaqabad, tel: 011-2692 5801; www.apollohospitaldelhi.com.

ETIQUETTE

Observing a few simple rules of etiquette will help to ensure a problem-free stay:

• Before entering someone's house, or a temple or mosque, it is essential to remove your shoes.

• Physical contact between men and women should be avoided. Men should not shake hands with a woman (unless she first offers to).

• Avoid taking leather goods of any kind into temples as these can often cause offence.

• For visits to places of worship, modest clothing is essential. In mosques, women should cover their head and arms and wear a long skirt.

• When eating with your fingers, remember to use only the right hand.

• Avoid pointing the soles of your feet towards anyone as this is considered a sign of disrespect.

• The central government has passed a law banning smoking in all public places, although the ban is only occasionally enforced.

G

GAY AND LESBIAN TRAVELLERS

Although only recently legalized, homosexuality is increasingly accepted, particularly among the urban young. Useful web resources for gay contacts and info on the Delhi gay scene include: GayDelhi (http://gaydelhi.tripod.com/) and Indian Dost (www.indiandost.com).

The only long-standing gay venue in Delhi is 'Pegs and Pints' on a Tuesday night; it is located behind Chanakya Cinema in the diplomatic district of Chanakyapuri. It is usually very crowded by 11pm but closes by 1am.

The lesbian scene in Delhi is even less evolved than the gay male scene, with the internet being the only valuable source of information. Try the lesbian support group and dating service, Sangini (http://members.tripod.com/~datingservice/sangini.html).

GETTING TO DELHI

Delhi has good international flight connections to other parts of Asia, Europe and the United States, as well as rapidly improving domestic links, a result of the continuing boom in budget airlines. The array of overland options is similarly broad, although overlanding from Europe to India with your own transport is still the preserve of a very determined few.

By air. Indira Gandhi Airport handles all international and domestic flights in and out of Delhi (see page 115).

For international flights, try online agencies such as www.expedia.com, www.cheapflights.com or www.flights4less.co.uk, or an India specialist such as www.southalltravel.co.uk for the most competitive rates.

Domestic airlines prioritise cost and going direct to their websites may get you exceptionally good rates, particularly well in advance. The longest established airlines, generally the most reliable but not usually the cheapest, are the state-run Indian Airlines (www.indian-airlines.nic.in) and Jet Airways/JetLite (www.jetairways.com). These have an Indian rupee rate for residents of India, and a substantially higher dollar rate for foreigners and NRIs (Non-Resident Indians).

The new budget airlines, however, make no such distinction, with one flat rate for all passengers, aiming to make air travel competitive with the highest train fares. The main players are: Air India Express (www.airindiaexpress.in); Deccan Airlines (www.deccanairlines.in); Go Air (www.goair.in); IndiGo Airlines (book.goindigo.in); Kingfisher Airlines (www.flykingfisher.com); Paramount Airways (www.paramountairways.com); SpiceJet (www.spicejet.com).

By train. Delhi's two main railway stations, New Delhi and Old Delhi, handle the vast majority of train traffic in and out of the city, although there are a number of smaller stations, most notably Hazrat Nizamuddin, near Humayun's tomb.

Rail travel is generally more comfortable than getting around by bus, though delays are common. Full timetables are available online at Indian Railways' website www.indianrail.gov.in, which also has details of the various classes available on each train.

There are seven different classes in total, although it's rare to find more than three or four types available on any one train. In descending order of price and comfort, they are: first class AC (very comfortable, air conditioned, with lockable cabins of two or four berths each); AC II tier (air-conditioned, with partitions arranged in groups of six berths with curtains that pull across to provide privacy); AC III tier (air-conditioned, with partitions of groups of nine berths; the middle berths fold down for sleeping); AC chair car (or 'CC';

reclining seats in air-conditioned carriages); first class non-AC (increasingly rare; not air-conditioned, but with ceiling fans, and lockable cabins of four or two berths each); sleeper class (partitions of nine berths with ceiling fans); and second class unreserved, with no berths and hard seats. Reservations are required for all classes other than second class unreserved. In the summer months it is best to go AC. All carriages have both Western and Indian-style toilets.

A booking office for foreign visitors is on the first floor of New Delhi Railway Station. The whole process will be significantly speedier if you know the number of the train you would like to travel on. It's also now possible to book tickets online at www.irctc.co.in using foreign credit cards, meaning that you can sort out your train tickets before you even arrive in India. You can book up to 60 days in advance and you'll be issued with an airline-style e-ticket to present onboard; you'll also need to show some form of photo ID such as a passport. However, the site is notoriously unreliable, and you'll be better off booking through the private, and much more efficient alternative, ClearTrip (www.cleartrip.com), which levies a Rs150 fee on all tickets. It's worth noting that ClearTrip also handle flight bookings for all the major domestic carriers.

By bus. There are thousands of buses connecting Delhi with every town and city of any importance for hundreds of miles in every direction. Rail travel is generally more comfortable, but buses take over in some places where train services are patchy or non-existent. The choice is usually between rust-bucket state buses, which are generally slow and uncomfortable, and the faster and much more comfortable private 'deluxe' services; tickets for these are sold by travel agents all over town. Most state-run buses leave from the Maharana Pratap ISBT by Kashmiri Gate metro; private buses usually depart from near the Ramakrishna Mission at the end of the Main Bazaar in Pahar Ganj.

GUIDES AND TOURS

Delhi tours. If you're pressed for time, joining a sightseeing tour of Delhi makes a lot of sense. There are a number of operators offering similar routes, the most dependable being those from the India Tourism Office at 88 Janpath (see page 131) or the Delhi Tourism & Transport Corporation office at the Coffee House, 1 Annexe, Emporium Complex, Baba Kharak Singh Marg opposite the Hanuman Mandir, tel: 011-6539 0009. For a more intimate experience, try Hotel Broadway (see page 133) or the Master Paying Guesthouse (see page 138). The Broadway offers a gastronomic walking tour of Old Delhi, while the very knowledgeable owner of the Master Paying Guesthouse promises to show you parts of Delhi most visitors don't see.

Other firms worth considering include the popular Delhi Heritage Walks (www.delhiheritagewalks.com), which offer guided walks around historic parts of the city, and the excellent Salaam Baalak Trust (www.salaambaalaktrust.com), who run off-beat walking tours of New Delhi Railway Station and environs by former street kids – a window on an otherwise hidden underbelly of the city's life.

Further afield. There are hundreds of travel agents offering tours to Agra and other destinations around Delhi. Rao Travels (tel: 011 2614 4949; www.raotravels.com) offers a day tour that takes in the Taj Mahal, Agra Fort and Fatehpur Sikri.

H

HEALTH AND MEDICAL CARE

The best way to ensure a healthy stay in Delhi is to prepare well in advance and then follow some simple guidelines once you're there. No vaccinations are legally required to enter the country, but your doctor is likely to recommend a few strongly, including typhoid, hepatitis and tetanus. There's also a slight potential risk of malaria, particularly if you are visiting just before, during or just after the monsoon – consult your doctor or a recognised travel health clinic for the latest advice.

Many of the afflictions most commonly suffered by visitors to Delhi can be easily avoided by following some simple guidelines:

• Never drink the tap water, not even when brushing your teeth; use bottled water instead, and avoid ice at all costs.

• Keep well hydrated at all times – try to drink even if you don't feel thirsty.

• Avoid food that's been reheated or left out in the open. Also avoid fresh fruit and salads unless you are sure they've been washed with clean water.

• Do everything you can to avoid getting bitten by mosquitoes – apply DEET-based repellent regularly, or better still stay covered up in the evenings, when they are more prevalent.

Delhi belly. The most common ailment suffered by overseas visitors is the notorious 'Delhi belly'. While this is caused partly by eating un-hygienically prepared food, it is as much a case of your stomach needing time to adjust to a range of ingredients with which it is wholly unfamiliar. Try to introduce new foods slowly, eating little and often, rather than bombarding your digestive system with too much too soon.

Should you succumb to an upset stomach, and/or the diarrhoea that often accompanies it, the best cure is to lay off food altogether for 24 hours, while drinking plenty of fluids, including rehydration salts, which are available from most pharmacies – 'Electrol' is the most common brand. Should symptoms persist, seek medical help. This is best arranged through your hotel; if all else fails, the best hospital in town is the Apollo, on Mathura Road, tel: 011-2692 5801.

L

LANGUAGE

Hindi is the official national language of India, but each state also has its own regional language. People in Delhi generally speak Hindi, but English is still used alongside Hindi for official purposes, while myriad regional languages are also widely spoken. Check out *Berlitz: Hindi Phrase Book & Dictionary* and *Berlitz: Hindi in 60 Minutes* (www.berlitzpublishing.com). The following are some useful words and expressions in Hindi:

hello/goodbye	**namaste**
yes	**ha**
no	**nahi**
How much?	**Kitna paisa?**
How far is the Jama Masjid?	**Jama Masjid kitna dur hai?**
thank you	**dhanyawad** (Hindu)/**shukriya** (Muslim)
I don't understand	**nahi samajta hai**
Do you speak English?	**English bolta?**
My name is (Sunil).	**mera naam (Sunil) hai.**

MAPS

The best map of Delhi is the Eicher map, which is available in both foldable paper and book form. Locals tend to navigate by landmarks rather than street names, which they may not know at all. Hospitals and cinemas are the most popular terms of reference. A passable map of Delhi is available from the tourist information desk in the arrivals hall of the international airport.

MEDIA

There are a massive number of newspapers available in Delhi, including both local and national dailies and weeklies. The most popular papers are the *Times of India* (www.timesofindia.indiatimes.com) and the *Hindustan Times* (www.hindustantimes.com), although *The*

Hindu (www.hinduonline.com) is widely regarded as the most cerebral. There are several excellent local *Time/Newsweek*-style weekly magazines, including *Outlook* (www.outlookindia.com), *India Today* (http://indiatoday.intoday.in), *Frontline* (www.frontlineonnet.com) and *Tehelka* (www.tehelka.com) – the last is particularly well known for its crusading investigative journalism. For entertainment listings, the best bets are *First City*, *Delhi City*, *Delhi Diary* and *City Limits*.

Most hotels will have access to news TV channels such as NDTV, Times Now (a collaboration between the *Times of India* and Reuters), BBC World and CNN, as well as assorted Star TV channels (Asia's answer to Sky).

MONEY

Currency. The monetary unit is the Indian rupee, divided into 100 paise. 1, 2 and 5 rupee coins are available, as well as 5, 10, 20, 50, 100, 500 and 1,000 rupee notes. Getting small change is a perennial problem. Be particularly conscious of this when changing money, as large notes can be a real headache to actually use. Notes with the smallest physical imperfection, a slight hole or tear, will be summarily refused; getting rid of such undesirable notes is something of a national pastime.

Banks and exchange. Major foreign currencies and travellers' cheques can be exchanged at most banks, although this tends to be a somewhat long-winded process, necessitating the filling in of a large number of forms. A better alternative is to go to a private money changer, which often have longer opening hours, more competitive rates and a quicker turnaround time. In an emergency, most top-end hotels will change money, though usually at poor rates.

Credit and debit cards. Credit cards are becoming an increasingly common method of payment in Delhi. Visa and MasterCard are widely accepted; American Express less so. However, shops will often add a surcharge over the cash rate if you pay by card, and you should keep as close an eye as possible on your card as it goes through the payment process, especially if the old-fashioned paper-docket machine is used, as credit-card fraud can be a problem.

ATMs. ATMs are now found everywhere in Delhi, normally in guarded, air-conditioned rooms next to the banks themselves. There are drawbacks to being wholly reliant on plastic, however, and you are well advised to have some cash or travellers' cheques with you as a fallback in case you lose the card, or have it swallowed by a cash machine. Make sure you make a note of your card number and the issuing bank's contact details before you leave home; and let your bank know you'll be travelling to India so it doesn't freeze your card the first time it's used as a security precaution.

O

OPENING TIMES

While some establishments shut later than others, nowhere opens early. Even government office hours vary, but 10am–6pm is a good rule of thumb. Lunch hours are rigidly observed, and the arrival of a cup of *chai* will signal a pause in proceedings no matter how urgent the case in hand. Museums and galleries are generally closed on Monday.

While most offices open Monday to Saturday, shops will normally close for one day a week according to the market in which they're located.

P

POLICE

Delhi has a dedicated squad of tourist police, based at various locations around the city. In an emergency, call 100. If you have to deal with the city's regular police, be as polite as possible, and don't be surprised to be asked for *baksheesh* (a bribe). Should you need to get a theft reported for insurance purposes, for example, you are unlikely to manage to do so without a small donation being made to the officer in question. This is often the only way that the police and other public workers can supplement their meagre incomes. Rs200–300 should normally get things moving, although much larger sums may be requested.

POST OFFICES

The Main GPO is on a large roundabout known as Gole Dakhana at the intersection of Baba Khark Singh Marg and Ashok Road. Its opening hours are 10am–1pm and 1.30–5pm Mon–Sat, and 10am–1pm Sun. For all other services, the post office in Connaught Place's A Block is likely to be more convenient. Postage rates are extremely reasonable. Consider using the 'Speed Post' service if your delivery is in any way urgent.

PUBLIC HOLIDAYS

Public holidays with fixed dates are:

26 January	Republic Day
15 August	Independence Day
2 October	Gandhi's Birthday
25 December	Christmas Day

Precise dates of religious festivals are calculated according to astrological and lunar calendars, and are therefore subject to change. Public holidays with movable dates are:

February/March	Holi
March/April	Good Friday
March/April	Ram Navami
May	Buddha Jayanti
September/October	Dussehra
October/November	Diwali (Deepavali)
November/December	Guru Nanak's Birthday

There are also four important Islamic festivals – Ramadan, Id ul-Fitr, Id ul-Zuha and Muharram – which follow the Islamic lunar calendar, falling around 11 days earlier year on year in the Western calendar.

PUBLIC TRANSPORT

With private car ownership still beyond the means of the average Delhiite, myriad possibilities exist for getting around town.

Metro. Delhi's modern and ever-expanding metro system (www.delhimetrorail.com) provides a fast, clean and convenient way of getting around parts of the city – see the Delhi metro map on pages 142–3 for city centre stations. Fares vary according to the length of the journey, ranging between Rs6 and Rs15. The line of most interest to the visitor is likely to be the one in and out of Old Delhi – an area so congested that access by road can be a real battle, making the metro the perfect alternative.

Taxis. Distinguishable by their black, yellow and green livery and yellow number plates, Delhi's taxis are generally difficult to flag down on the street. They gather at their transport company's kiosk, which can be found close to all the main markets or commercial areas. Rates are meant to be determined by meter, though a little persuasion is often required to ensure their use, drivers preferring to fix a rate before departure. A 25 percent surcharge is added at night.

One way to avoid any haggling over fares is to opt for a pre-paid taxi, where you pay in advance at a dedicated counter then present the chit to the driver. This service is available at the airports, and New Delhi Railway station.

The best alternative for new arrivals is to arrange a radio cab. These charge around 10 percent more than a regular taxi (or 25 percent at night), but are worth the extra. The cars tend to be newer, better maintained, air-conditioned and comfortable, with more boot room.

The following radio cab firms are all dependable (remember, national callers have to prefix city code of +011 and international callers have to put country code +091and city code +011.

Mega Cab: 1929, 41414141

Delhi Cab: 44333222

Metro Cab: 1923

Rickshaws. These are generally of the 'auto' variety (motorised three-wheelers), although cycle (pedal-powered) rickshaws still operate in Old Delhi elsewhere – despite repeated attempts by the municipality to outlaw. Autos represent the most convenient way of making longer trips across the city, if not the most comfortable. They converge on street corners, but can be flagged down from the kerb. As with taxis, meters should be used but seldom are – negotiate a price before setting off.

Buses. Since the introduction of brand new, air-conditioned, low-floor buses by the Delhi Transport Corporation, travelling by bus in the capital has been transformed. The fleet, in eye-catching green, is cleaner, more environmentally friendly and infinitely more comfortable than before, with dedicated lanes on congestion prone routes.

In addition, a smaller fleet of state-of-the-art 'cluster buses' was also launched in 2011, complete with on-board, real-time travel info.

T

TELEPHONE

The area code for Delhi is 011, and the country code for India +91. This means that calls to Delhi from abroad should be prefixed with +91 11 and then the eight-digit number. Numbers change regularly; the latest revisions mean that any number you see starting with a 5 is now likely to start with a 4 instead.

Public phone booths are generally yellow and marked 'STD' (Standard Trunk Dialling) to denote national calls, and 'ISD' (International Subscriber Dialling) for international.

Delhi has wholeheartedly embraced mobile-phone culture. Since the terror attacks of 2008, however, the government has made it more difficult for foreigners to access Indian networks using a pre-paid SIM card. You'll be required to fill in forms and provide photos, as well as photocopies of your passport/visa. Any mobile phone shop in the city will help you get up and running, although it may take a day or two for your SIM to work. The major incentive to do this is that Indian mobile charges are considerably cheaper than elsewhere.

TIME ZONES

Indian Standard Time is 5.5 hours ahead of GMT all year round.

TIPPING

Hotel staff should be tipped for duties such as baggage carrying or room service. Rs10 or 20 is normally sufficient, although staff in five-star properties may have become accustomed to more. It's normal to leave a tip of 10 percent or so at the end of a meal in a restaurant, assuming that service has not been included in the bill.

TOILETS

The Public Works Department in charge of public toilets, Sulabh, has some well-maintained facilities in certain parts of the city, less so in others. Users will be charged a Rs2 entrance fee, and the toilets will generally be of the Indian design.

TOURIST INFORMATION

Delhi's most helpful and informative tourist office is the one run by India Tourism Delhi at 88 Janpath (tel: 011-2332 0008). There are 24-hour desks at both airports, which dispense free maps, provide basic information and can help with hotel bookings.

Be very wary of other offices claiming to offer official tourist information, particularly those in Pahar Ganj and Connaught Place. They are simply travel agents out to ensnare unsuspecting tourists, and should be strenuously avoided if you simply need information.

VISAS AND ENTRY REQUIREMENTS

Nationals of all countries except Nepal and Bhutan require a visa to enter India. Standard multiple-entry tourist visas are valid for six months from date of issue, and are available from any Indian Embassy, High Commission or Consulate worldwide.

Indian Customs allows nationals other than those from neighbouring states to bring 200 cigarettes, 50 cigars or 250g of tobacco into India, as well as 1 litre of wine or spirits. Visitors can bring as much currency into the country as they like, but are not permitted to take any rupees out of the country without government clearance.

WEBSITES AND INTERNET ACCESS

Accessing the internet is no problem in Delhi, although finding a comfortable place to do so, with a reliable connection, can be more tricky. There are a number of reasonable places around Connaught Place; look out for the red 'Sify' internet centres – they tend to be more professional than most. Most places will let you download digital photos, burn CDs and make phone calls over the net.
Useful websites are:
www.delhitourism.com Official government website
www.newdelhihub.com and www.delhigate.com Both useful for general information
www.exploredelhi.com Information on more cultural pursuits
www.delhilive.com Listings of current events

YOUTH HOSTELS

There are three youth hostels in Delhi, all run to a good standard and well located, if not particularly cheap. The YMCA Tourist Hostel on Jai Singh Road, just south of Connaught Place (www.newdelhiymca. org), has 120 rooms and dormitories covering a wide range of budgets, while the YWCA (www.ywcaindia.org), close by on Sansad Marg, is smaller and cosier; both offer accommodation to men and women. The other option is the Youth Hostel at 5 Naya Marg in Chanakyapuri, a much more peaceful location.

Recommended Hotels

Delhi's hotels regularly sell out during the winter season, so if you are coming between September and March be sure to book ahead. Bear in mind that many of the more expensive hotels offer their best rates online. While there are plenty of options at the upper and lower ends of the scale, reasonable mid-range accommodation can be a struggle to find – at least, close to the centre. The rates given here are for a double room without taxes – expect to pay up to 20 percent more once 'luxury' and 'service' taxes have been added. For youth hostels, see page 132.

$$$$$	over Rs10,000
$$$$	Rs6,000–10,000
$$$	Rs3,000–6,000
$$	Rs1,000–3,000
$	under Rs1,000

OLD DELHI/CIVIL LINES

Hotel Broadway $$$$ *4/15A Asaf Ali Road, tel: 2327 3821, www. hotelbroadwaydelhi.com.* The 32 rooms are clean if nothing special, but the hotel's restaurant, Chor Bizarre, and Thug's bar make this an interesting place to stay on the boundaries of New and Old Delhi. The hotel also offers an excellent 'gastronomic' tour of the area.

Oberoi Maidens Hotel $$$$$ *7 Sham Nath Marg, tel: 2397 5464, www.maidenshotel.com.* A classic Raj-era hotel with oodles of period character, the Maidens first opened its doors in 1903 and was where visiting VIPs used to stay before the advent of Lutyen's New Delhi. This explains its slightly off-centre location near Kashmiri Gate – an area that's peaceful at night and, being mid-way between Old and New Delhi, well placed for sightseeing (the nearest metro station is only a five-minute walk away). Elegant, high-ceilinged rooms, and an 8-acre garden.

Wongdhen House $ *15A New Tibetan Colony, Manju-ka-Tilla, tel: 2381 2896, email: 2wongdhenhouse@gmail.com.* About 2km (1.25 miles) north of Old Delhi, this predominantly Tibetan colony offers a more peaceful range of backpacker accommodation than Pahar Ganj. This place is by far the most popular establishment, offering a soothing atmosphere and clean, well-priced rooms – though bring plenty of mosquito repellent.

CONNAUGHT PLACE

HK Choudhary Guest House $$ *H-35/3 Connaught Circus, tel: 4350 9878, www.indiamart.com/hkchoudharyguesthouse.* Cramped but clean and friendly hotel, in a very central location with an exceptionally helpful manager. Can be a slight struggle to find – it's very tucked away down a back lane.

Hans Plaza $$$$$ *15 Barakhamba Road (16th–20th floors), tel: 6615 0000, www.hanshotels.com.* Boutique hotel at a prime location, in a tower block just off Connaught Circus. The designer furnishings and fittings are showing signs of wear but this is still one of the best value places in its class. If you're planning to sleep your jet lag off here, go for a quieter 'superior' room higher up the building. Superb views from the top-floor restaurant.

Hotel Fifty Five $$$ *H-55 Connaught Place, tel: 2332 1244, www. hotel55.com.* Fifteen small but spotless rooms (some windowless), in central if sometimes noisy location, pleasant roof terrace for breakfast. Friendly staff.

Imperial Hotel $$$$$ *Janpath, tel: 2334 1234, www.theimperial india.com.* Delhi's premier hotel is a superb Art Deco building dating from the twilight of the Raj, in a very central location just off Connaught Circus. The overriding impression is one of old-world elegance: the whitewashed facade flanked by tall palm trees yields to interiors of cream walls and Burmese teak, gleaming Italian marble floors and sparkling chandeliers. The rooms are plush without being showy and the courtyard pool is a welcome haven.

Metropolitan Hotel $$$$$ *Bangla Sahib Road, tel: 4250 0200, http://hotelmetdelhi.com.* This gleaming, modern business hotel is an exceptionally well-run place, with distinctly un-Indian levels of efficiency. There's a top notch health spa, fitness centre and swimming pool, and the best Japanese restaurant in town (Sakura).

The Park $$$$$ *15 Sansad Marg, tel: 2374 3000, www.theparkhotels. com.* Some of the funkiest contemporary-style rooms in town, with designer interiors, plus an award-winning Indian gourmet-fusion restaurant (Fire), glamorous poolside bar and great location overlooking the Jantar Mantar; the freshest of the major five stars.

Ringo Guest House $ *17 Scindia House, Connaught Lane (off Janpath), tel: 2331 0605, email: ringoguesthouse@yahoo.co.in.* The pick of the backpacker options in Connaught Place, Ringo's has tiny but well-scrubbed rooms, a passable restaurant and friendly staff.

PAHAR GANJ AND AROUND

This area is Delhi's main backpacker haunt, with the cheapest and best value accommodation in town, as well as a range of cheap cafés selling the usual travellers' staples. It's a congested, tight-knit area which can be quite a shock to the senses of first-time visitors, but is easily the best place to meet other travellers.

Ajanta $$–$$$ *36 Arakashan Road, Ram Nagar, tel: 2956 2057, www. ajantahotel.com.* Slightly away from the Main Bazaar area, this is one of the more upmarket options in Pahar Ganj, offering great value. Its marble-floored rooms are spacious and well maintained, and there's a good range of facilities, including a restaurant, travel desk and baggage storage. They do free airport transfers too, and offer discounts of stays of two nights or more.

Ajay $$ *5084A Main Bazaar, tel: 2358 3125, www.anupamhoteliersltd. com.* Part of a group that also includes the nearby Anoop and Hare Krishna hotels, this place is a backpacker institution in Delhi. Offering some of the most competitively priced accommodation in the city, it's popular as much for its excellent bakery and rooftop terrace restaurant (where open fires are lit in the evenings) and for its rooms, which vary greatly in size and standards of cleanliness.

Grand Godwin $$–$$$ *41 Arakashan Road, Ram Nagar, tel: 2354 6791, www.godwinhotels.com.* One of the best mid-range options in the area, slightly removed from the main Pahar Ganj bazaar in a relatively quiet side street and offering well-equipped a/c rooms with marble floors, TV and fridge, plus a multi-cuisine restaurant.

Rak International $ *820 Main Bazaar, Chowk Baoli, tel: 2358 6508, www.hotelrakinternational.com.* An enduringly popular rock-bottom option off the Main Bazaar in a small square. It's clean and quiet for the price, with well kept, good-sized rooms and a relaxing rooftop restaurant.

ELSEWHERE IN NEW DELHI

The Ambassador $$$$$ *Sujan Singh Park, Cornwallis Road, tel: 2463 2600, www.tajhotels.com.* In a whitewashed period building close to Khan Market shopping complex (one of Delhi's best), this place has a less haughty air than some of the other upmarket hotels, plus a range of quirky bars and restaurants, but no swimming pool.

Claridges $$$$$ *12 Aurangzeb Road, tel: 4133 5133, www.claridges-hotels.com.* Beautiful colonial building in a smart part of town, set amid its own landscaped grounds, boasting elegant fin-de-siècle interiors, attentive service and a refined atmosphere. International-grade facilities include a gorgeous spa, ultra-chic bar and a couple of fine-dining restaurants, including one (Dhaba) with a reconstructed Indian Tata truck as part of the décor.

Home Away from Home (aka 'New Delhi Bed and Breakfast') **$$$** *D-8 Gulmohar Park (1st floor), tel: 2689 4812, email: permkamte@ sify.com.* This delightful homestay, hosted by Renu Dayal, for once really docs offer a homely ambience, with just two nicely furnished rooms in a quiet, leafy area. The owners are extremely hospitable and offer discounts for longer stays. Meals are served by arrangement, and guests get the run of a flower-filled garden patio. Tariffs include breakfast.

La Sagrita $$$ *14 Sunder Nagar, tel: 2435 9541, www.lasagrita.com.* Another good option in this upscale government area, La Sagrita is a cosy, modern and comfortable midscale hotel, popular mainly with independent foreign travellers. All the rooms are air-conditioned and have their own private terraces and small kitchenette areas, and there's also an immaculately kept garden to relax in.

Oberoi $$$$$ *Dr Zakir Hussain Marg, tel: 2436 3030, www.oberoi hotels.com.* Despite the unprepossessing exterior, this luxurious property manages to exude an air of grandeur which no other hotel can quite match. The public areas are fastidiously well maintained, the rooms finished to a high standard, and the flagship restaurant, Threesixty, is by some margin the classiest in the city.

Shangri-La's Eros $$$$$ *19 Ashoka Road, Connaught Place, tel: 4119 1919, www.shangri-la.com.* Amazing panoramic views over Lutyen's New Delhi unfold from the upper floors of the Shangri La's Eros, a five-star occupying a floodlit skyscraper, close to the capital's principal landmark, India Gate. The lobby's a dazzling expanse of polished marble and crystal chandeliers, and there's a wide choice of multicuisine restaurants, a large curviform pool in the garden, in-house art gallery and luxury spa to help ease the jet lag.

Shervani $$$–$$$$ *11 Sunder Nagar, tel: 4250 1000, www.shervani hotels.com.* Set in a convenient location in smart Sunder Nagar, this extremely stylish modern hotel offers well-equipped rooms complete with flat-screen TV, broadband connection, minibar and 'mood lighting', and there's a smart little in-house café-restaurant. Their standard rooms offer particularly good value.

Taj Mahal $$$$$ *1 Mansingh Road, tel: 2302 6162, www.tajhotels. com.* More central than the other five-star Taj properties, this luxury hotel offers all the usual amenities, but with a dash of character. There's a bar, Rick's, and a 24-hour restaurant, which is one of the city's best late-night options.

KAROL BAGH AND AROUND

Bajaj Indian Home Stay $$$ *8A/34 WEA, Karol Bagh, tel: 2573 6509, www.bajajindianhomestay.com.* Promising an experience that's

'Indian, altogether', this place prides itself on its homely ambience, treating each guest as one of their own. It certainly stands out from the crowd, and the rooms are spotlessly clean.

Good Times Hotel $$$ *8/7 WEA Karol Bagh, off Pusa Road, tel: 2875 6001, www.goodtimeshotel.com.* Presentable rooms, a pleasant rooftop restaurant and convenient location. The staff seem permanently rushed off their feet, but then this is one of the better-value places around, so be sure to book early.

Master Paying Guesthouse $$$ *R-500 New Rajender Nagar (Shankar and GR Hospital Road crossing), tel: 2874 1089, www.master-guesthouse.com.* Small but exquisitely well decorated and managed, this is one place where attention to detail is second to none. The extremely knowledgeable owners, Avnish and Ushi, put their heart and soul into the place, and also offers fascinating walking tours of 'hidden Delhi'.

Yatri House $$$ *Corner of Panchkuin and Mandir Margs, tel: 2362 5563, www.yatrihouse.com.* Set back down a lane from a busy main road, this is a welcoming, efficiently run, guesthouse in a modern family home, with a leafy garden out front and brick courtyard to the rear. The rooms are immaculate and tariffs include airport pick up and drop, complementary teas and afternoon samosas. Despite the uninspiring locale, it's only 1km (just over 0.5 mile) from Connaught Place.

SOUTH DELHI

The Grand $$$$$ *Nelson Mandela Road, Vasant Kunj, tel: 2677 1234, www.thegrandnewdelhi.com.* The classy, contemporary design helps this property stand out from the bland five-star crowd. There's an interesting range of restaurants, including Japanese, and a great pool and health spa. It's very convenient for the airport, and the staff are extremely efficient.

Jaypee Vasant Continental $$$$$ *Basant Lok, Vasant Vihar, tel: 2614 8800, www.jaypeehotels.com.* Its contemporary styling and innovative eateries are this new luxury hotel's USPs. Located close to the airport but in an upmarket residential area, it has a great swimming pool, a lively bar, a couple of exceptional restaurants and a state-of-the-art spa. The staff are unfailingly courteous.

Jorbagh 27 $$$ *27 Jorbagh, tel: 2469 4430, www.jorbagh27.com.* Set in a residential area, but managed more as a hotel than a guesthouse, this 18-room property lacks some of the charm of the more 'homely' establishments, but is efficiently run, clean and well located, with the proximity of Lodi Gardens a real bonus.

Lutyens Bungalow $$$ *39 Prithviraj Road, tel: 2461 1341, www.lutyensbungalow.co.in.* Family-run guest house, housed in a 1930s mansion designed by the great architect himself. On one of New Delhi's most exclusive boulevards, the place oozes old-world gentility, with manicured lawns set behind high walls, and has a very friendly feel – though the real deal-sealer is their lovely garden pool. Be sure to book well in advance.

Manor $$$$ *77 Friends Colony (West), tel: 2692 5151, www. themanordelhi.com.* This contemporary-style luxury boutique hotel is the essence of understated elegance. Set in beautifully manicured gardens, tucked away from the bustle of the city, with a rooftop terrace that makes the perfect place to unwind after a hard day's sightseeing. The only downside: no pool.

AIRPORT AND GURGAON

Inn at Delhi $$$ *C-34 Anand Niketan, tel: 2411 3233.* Luxury B&B on the edge of the diplomatic enclave, surrounded on three sides by parks and mature trees. Tranquil and efficient, it offer large rooms for the price, all of them crammed with repro antiques and curios, and the hospitality is flawless.

Radisson $$$$$ *NH8, close to IGI Airport, tel: 2677 9191, www. radisson.com.* This smart-looking hotel has standard five-star accommodation, but the restaurants and coffee shop stand out from the crowd, and the bar has a remarkably long happy hour.

INDEX

Berlitz pocket guide

Delhi

Third Edition 2012

Written by Matt Barrett
Updated by David Abram
Edited by Sarah Sweeney
Series Editor: Tom Stainer
Production: Tynan Dean, Linton Donaldson
and Rebeka Ellam

All Rights Reserved
© 2012 Apa Publications (UK) Limited

Printed in China by CTPS

Berlitz Trademark Reg. U.S. Patent Office and other countries. Marca Registrada. Used under license from the Berlitz Investment Corporation

Photography credits: Fotolia 1, Henry Wilson, 2ML, 2/3T, 3TC, 2/3rd 4ML, 4MR, 6ML, 7MC, 7TC, 12, 13, 15, 16, 19, 26, 29, 30, 32, 35, 40, 42, 45, 46, 50, 51, 52, 56, 58, 59, 60, 61, 62, 65, 66, 70, 77, 79, 88, 90, 95, 96, 100 107; Bernard Castelein 21; Corbis 24; Danny Lehman/Corbis 8; Hulton Archive 21; Julian Love 2TL, 3ML, 4TL, 4/5M, 5MC, 4/5 6,5TC, 6TL, 6ML, 7MC, 17, 22, 33, 37, 39, 43, 44, 47, 49, 53, 55, 64, 68, 72, 74, 76, 80, 82, 84, 87, 92, 93, 99, 102, 104

Cover picture: 4Corners Images

Contact us

At Berlitz we strive to keep our guides as accurate and up to date as possible, but if you find anything that has changed, or if you have any suggestions on ways to improve this guide, then we would be delighted to hear from you.

Berlitz Publishing, PO Box 7910,
London SE1 1WE, England.
email: berlitz@apaguide.co.uk
www.insightguides.com/berlitz

Delhi Metro

Mundka
- Rajdhani Park
- Nangloi Station
- Nangloi
- Surajmal Stadium
- Udyog Nagar
- Peera Garhi
- Paschim Vihar (West)
- Paschim Vihar (East)
- Madi Pur
- Shivaji Park
- Punjabi Bagh

Rithala
- Rohini West
- Rohini East
- Kohat Enclave
- Netaji Subhash Place
- Keshav Puram
- Kanhaiya Nagar

Jahangirpuri
- Adarsh Nagar
- Azadpur
- Model Town
- GTB Nagar
- Vishwa Vidyalaya
- Vidhan Sabha
- Civil Lines

Badli
Sanjay Gandhi

Dilshad Garden
- Jhilmil
- Mansarovar Park
- Shahdara
- Welcome
- Seelampur

Vaishali
- Kaushambi
- Anand Vihar
- Karkar Duma
- Preet Vihar
- Nirman Vihar
- Laxmi Nagar

Ashok Park
- Satguru Ramsingh Marg
- Shadipur

Inderlok
- Shastri Nagar
- Pratap Nagar
- Pul Bangash
- Tis Hazari

Kashmere Gate
- Shastri Park
- Chandni Chowk
- Chawri Bazar

Kirti Nagar
- Moti Nagar
- Ramesh Nagar

New Delhi
- Patel Nagar East
- Rajendra Place
- Karol Bagh
- Jhandewalan
- RK Ashram Marg

Rajiv Chowk
- Barakhamba Road
- Mandi House
- Pragati Maidan
- Indraprastha
- Yamuna Bank

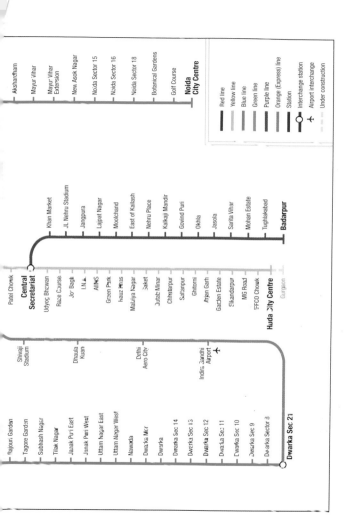

Berlitz®

speaking your language

phrase book & dictionary
phrase book & CD

Available in: Arabic, Cantonese Chinese, Croatian, Czech, Danish, Dutch, English*, Finnish*, French, German, Greek, Hebrew*, Hindi, Hungarian*, Indonesian, Italian, Japanese, Korean, Latin American Spanish, Mandarin Chinese, Mexican Spanish, Norwegian, Polish, Portuguese, Romanian*, Russian, Spanish, Swedish, Thai, Turkish, Vietnamese

*Book only

www.berlitzpublishing.com